The New Context of World Mission

Bryant L. Myers

MARC

a division of
World Vision International
800 West Chestnut Avenue
Monrovia, California 91016-3198 USA

The New Context of World Mission

Bryant L. Myers

Published by MARC, a division of World Vision International
800 West Chestnut Avenue
Monrovia, California 91016-3198 USA

Copyright © 1996 by MARC (Mission Advanced Research and Communications Center). All rights reserved. No portion of this book may be reproduced in any form, except for brief reviews, without the written permission of the publisher.

ISBN 1-887983-00-7

Printed in the United States of America. Designer: Richard Sears.

> **Slides and overheads available.** The graphic pages of this book are available as 35mm slides and overhead transparencies in full color. Please contact MARC for details.

a division of World Vision International
800 West Chestnut Avenue
Monrovia, California 91016-3198 USA

Contents

Introduction 4

The Historical Context of Mission

Changing paradigms of mission thinking 8
The unfolding of mission history 10
The Christian church grows serially 12
Christianity and Isalm: The ebb and flow 13

State of the World

The world by religion... 16
The poor and the lost.. 17
How are the childen?... 18
The world's poor 19
A world in conflict 20
People without borders 21
The world by population 22
The world by income 24
Global economic integration 26
Global technology and communications................ 27
Economic freedom 28
Structures of sin 29
The growing human family..................................... 30
Consuming the earth's resources 32
Who has not heard?... 33

The Church in the World

Shape of the Christian world................................... 36
State of the Christian church................................... 37
The church in Africa 38
The church in Asia 39
The church in Europe... 40
The church in Latin America 41
The status of the Great Commission 42

Challenges to Christian Mission

Who needs to hear?... 44
Children and youth.. 45
The growing cities in the south 46
The Muslim world.. 47
Allocating our resources for mission 48
The sinned-against 49
Complex humanitarian emergencies & refugees 50
The crucial importance of women 51
Promoting equitable human development.............. 52
Caring for creation 53

Conclusions.. 54
A biblical counterpoint 57

INTRODUCTION

The new context of world mission

God's world is undergoing profound, rapid, dizzying change at the close of the second millennium since the birth of his Son. Many agree that there have been few periods of history in which individuals, organizations and nations have faced changes on the current scale. Virtually every area of life is being tossed about, seemingly at the whim of forces far beyond our understanding and control. Economics, demographics, technology, the social and spiritual fabric of society, all are undergoing foundational change at a rate almost too fast to follow.

The last decades of this century have witnessed the breaking down of a world order that had been in place since the end of World War II. Early expectations that the post-Cold War period would see reduced levels of conflict and broader economic prosperity have been disappointed. Instead, the end of the second millennium is a time of great uncertainty and fear in many parts of the world. Hope for a better future seems threatened by a combination of spiritual, economic, political, cultural and environmental factors over which people feel little control.

There is some good news. Premier Christian researcher David Barrett points out that the proportion of Christians actively involved in some form of mission is at an all-time high of 36% and most Christian researchers agree that the number of unevangelized people in the world is declining, albeit slowly. There has been an unprecedented wave of human freedom sweeping across many lands. The 1995 United Nations Human Development Report claims that the speed of human development — measured in terms of health, education and economics — in the "developing" countries in the last three decades is three times faster than that of the industrialized world during the nineteenth century.

There is also a lot of disturbing news. There are still over one billion human beings living in places where it is unlikely they will ever hear the good news about Jesus Christ, unless someone goes to tell them. The Christian church continues to decline in places where it was once strong. Too many Christians, stubbornly holding onto the modern dichotomy between the material and the spiritual, limit the lordship of Christ to their inner, private lives. Countries whose populations are overwhelmingly Christian are suffering from corruption, ethnic violence, tolerance for the killing in the womb and unbridled consumption.

The world is a violent place, often inhospitable to human life. There are over 50 ongoing wars taking place as this book is being written. There are almost

INTRODUCTION

50 million uprooted people who have had to flee their homes because of violence, disaster, economics or a failing environment. There are one billion people who do not have access to the basic social services of health care, education, safe drinking water and adequate nutrition. The gap between those with more than enough and those who live on the margins of life is widening. The phenomenon of global economic integration is leaving some people and even some nations permanently on the sidelines.

The purpose of *The New Context of World Mission* is to provide a brief, easy to read, yet comprehensive description of the world in which Christian mission is to take place as this century closes. Understanding that people who make things happen have little time to study lengthy books, academic papers and tables of information, this booklet provides a bird's-eye view of the context of mission, while preserving some of the complexity of the world.

This booklet is intended to be both a revision and an expansion of *The Changing Shape of World Mission*. A few of the pages of *Changing Shape* have been updated with the best currently available information. Some pages have been changed completely. Many new pages have been added.

Because the context of Christian mission is a hurting, conflicted world stubbornly at odds with its Creator, some may feel that this booklet focuses too much on the "secular." This feeling needs to be resisted. Looking at the world needing Christ's mission means looking at the fallen material and spiritual parts of the world — a holistic view. This does not make the view any less Christian or biblical. It is after all God's world — all of it.

Jesus wept for a real Jerusalem, a Jerusalem ruled by Rome and entrapped by religiosity rooted in human rules, a Jerusalem of upper rooms, small shops, lepers, beggars, and rich young rulers, a Jerusalem of Pharisees who came at night, adulteresses and crowds of ordinary people who couldn't make up their minds, a Jerusalem so spiritually blind that it could not recognize the Messiah it longed for even when he stood in their midst. This is the context of Christian mission.

The Historical Context of Mission

THE HISTORICAL CONTEXT OF MISSION

Changing paradigms of mission thinking

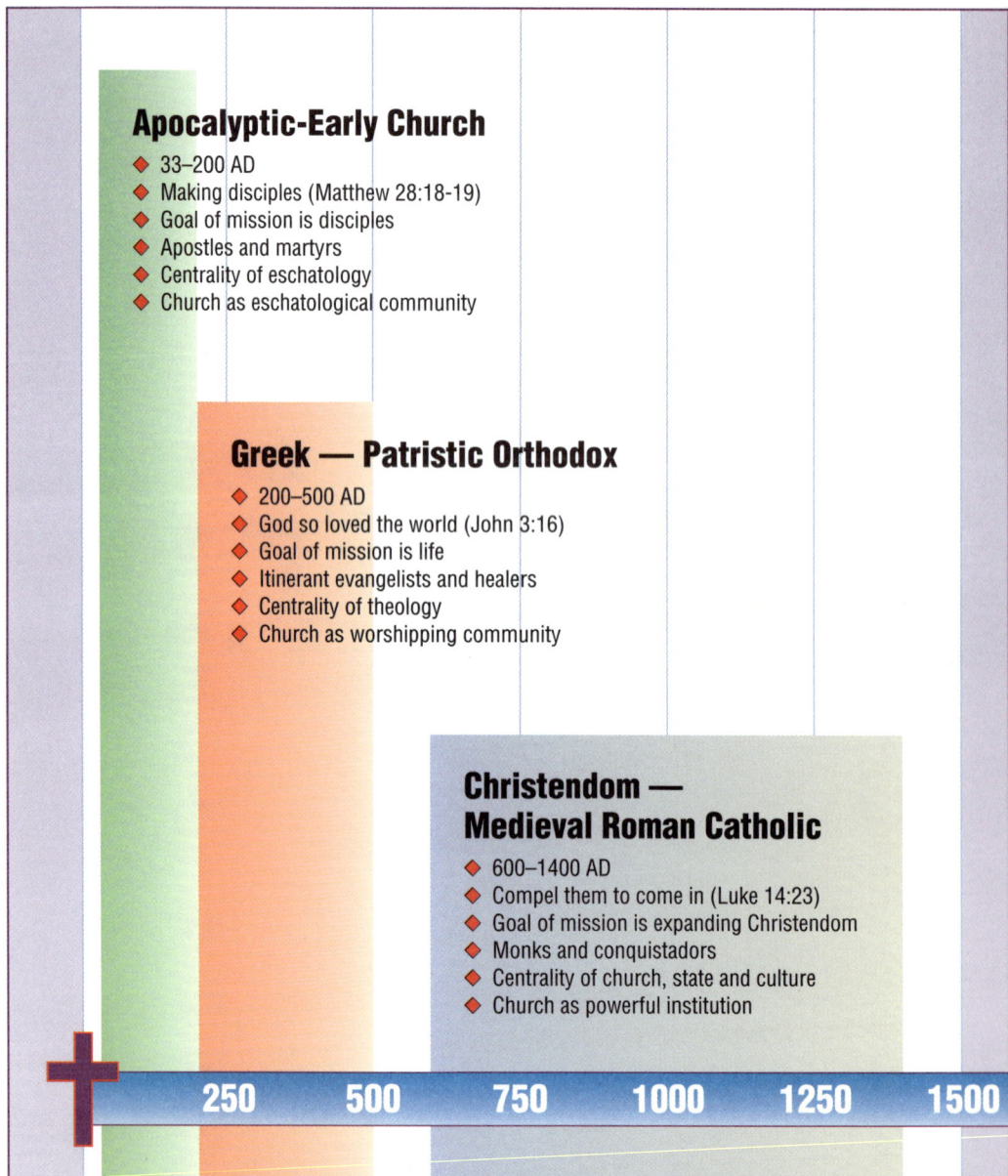

Apocalyptic-Early Church
- 33–200 AD
- Making disciples (Matthew 28:18-19)
- Goal of mission is disciples
- Apostles and martyrs
- Centrality of eschatology
- Church as eschatological community

Greek — Patristic Orthodox
- 200–500 AD
- God so loved the world (John 3:16)
- Goal of mission is life
- Itinerant evangelists and healers
- Centrality of theology
- Church as worshipping community

Christendom — Medieval Roman Catholic
- 600–1400 AD
- Compel them to come in (Luke 14:23)
- Goal of mission is expanding Christendom
- Monks and conquistadors
- Centrality of church, state and culture
- Church as powerful institution

Adapted from Bosch, *Transforming Mission*, Orbis, 1991

Reformation — Protestant
- 1500–1750 AD
- The gospel is the power of salvation for everyone who believes (Romans 1:16)
- Goal of mission is renewal
- Holy Spirit and reformed church
- Centrality of Scripture
- Church as reforming community

Modern Mission Era
- 1750–1950 AD
- Come over and help us (Acts 16:9)
- Goal is salvation / better life
- Volunteers, missionaries
- Centrality of mission task
- Church as civilizing (Westernizing) community

Emerging mission paradigm at the end of the second millenium
- 1950– ?
- They preached, drove out demons and healed them (Mark 6:12)
- Goal of mission is to call people to faith who then work for social and spiritual transformation
- All of the people of God in all of life
- Centrality of holism — life, deed, word and sign
- Church as pilgrim community

1500   1750   2000

THE HISTORICAL CONTEXT OF MISSION

The unfolding of mission history

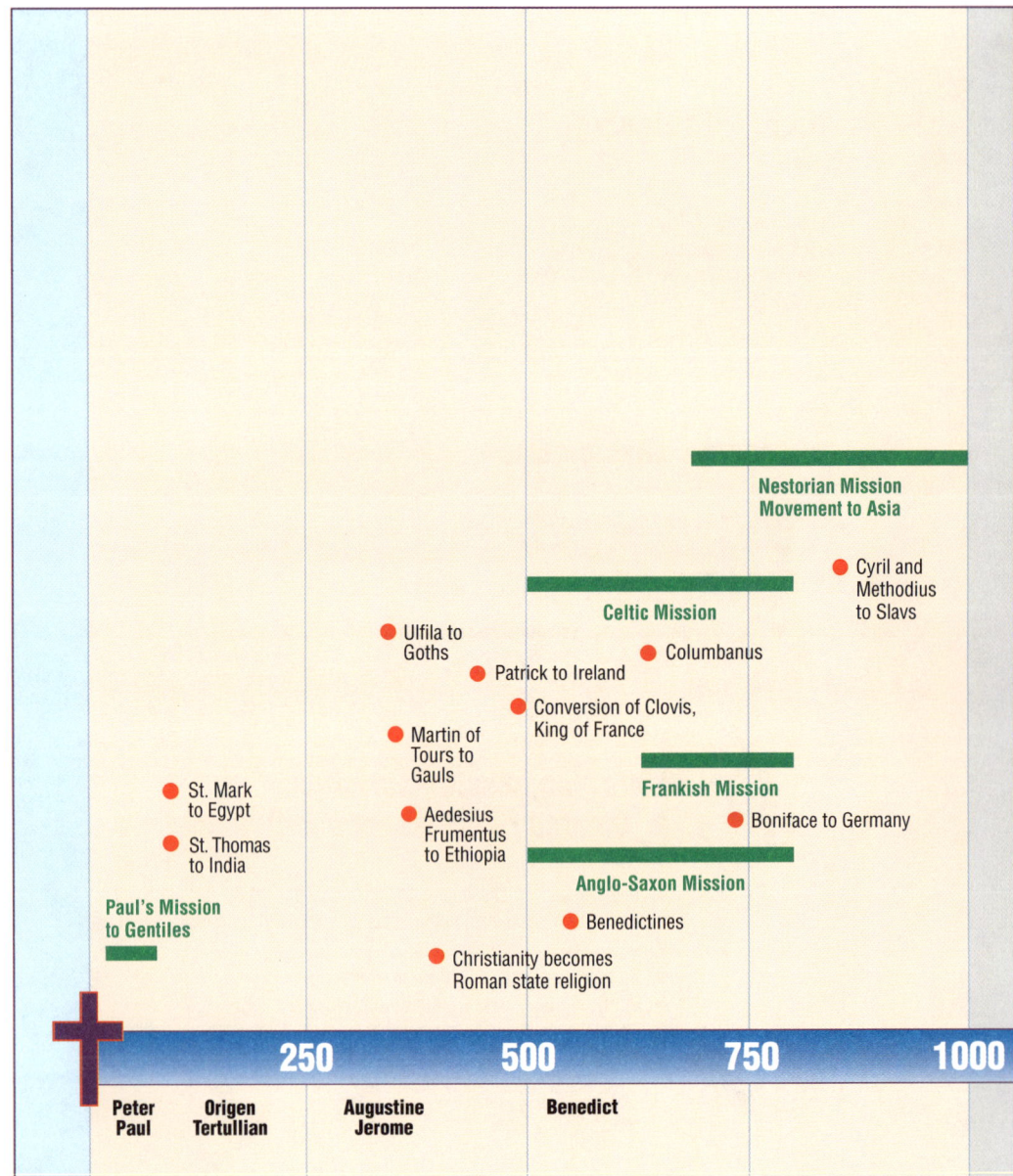

Developed from Neill, *A History of Christian Missions*, Penguin, 1964; Lapple, *The Catholic Church: A Brief History*, Paulist, 1982

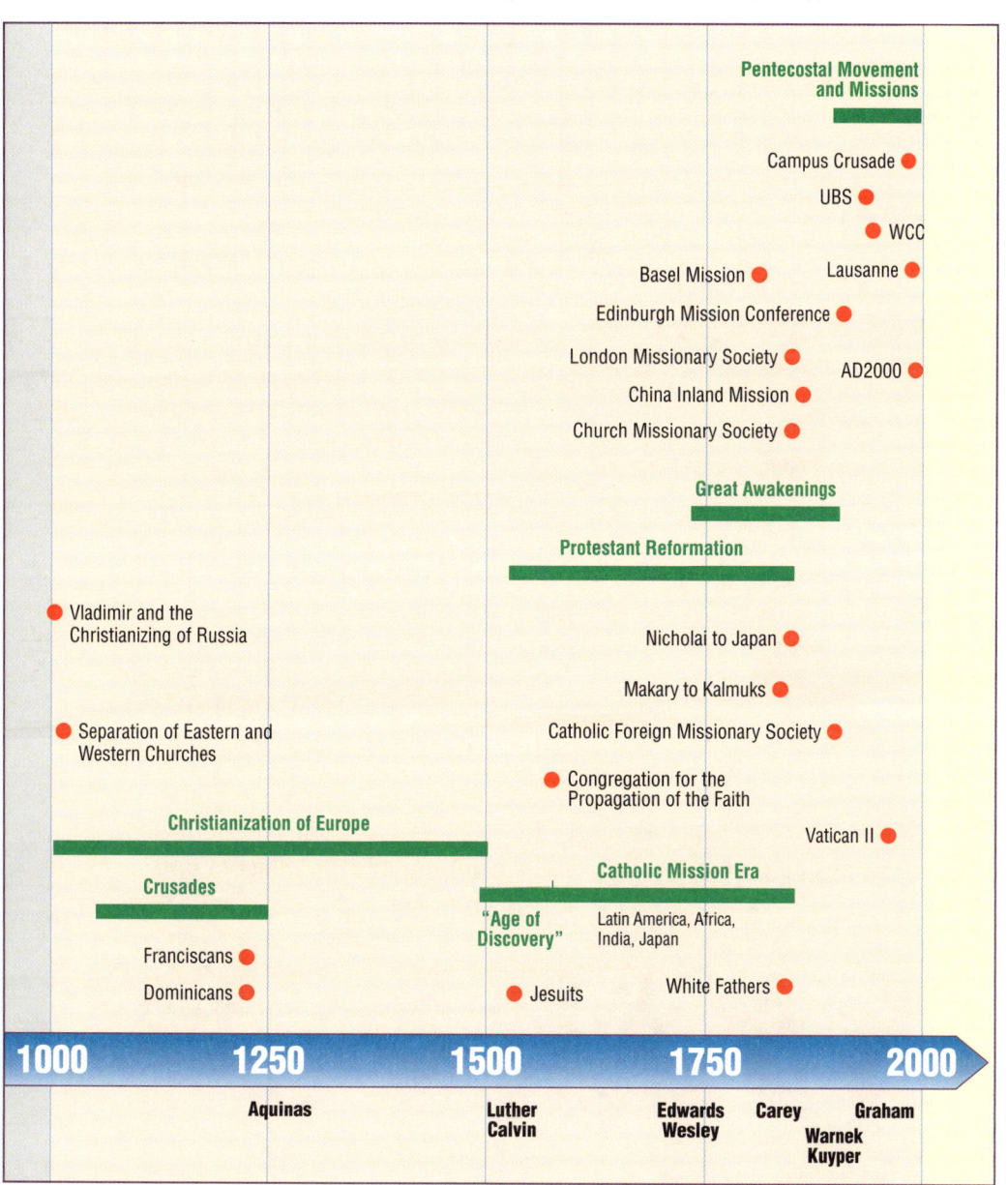

THE NEW CONTEXT OF WORLD MISSION 11

THE HISTORICAL CONTEXT OF MISSION

The Christian church grows serially

The Church in 100 AD

The Church in 400 AD

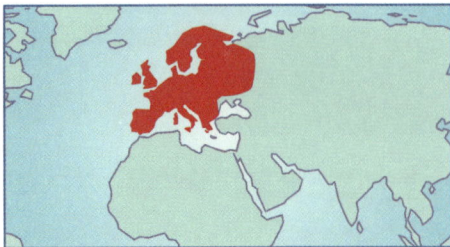
The Church in 1500 AD

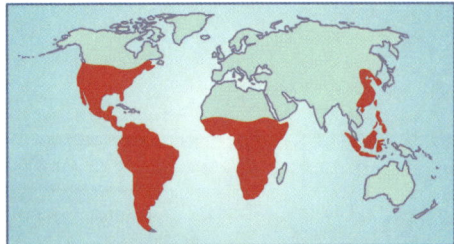
The Church in 1990 AD

- In the first century, the Christian church began as a Jewish church in Jerusalem and then moved to Western Asia, becoming a largely Gentile church with its center still in Jerusalem.

- By A.D. 600, the church spread to North Africa and to southern Europe. Its language was largely Greek. The center of gravity of the church lay between Rome and Constantinople.

- By A.D. 1000, the church had largely disappeared from North Africa and the Middle East in the face of a surging Islam. The center of gravity of the church now lay in Europe, which was largely Christian by A.D. 1500. Theology and mission became largely European.

- By the mid-twentieth century, the church had declined significantly in Europe and the center of gravity now lies in the Two-Thirds World — Latin America, Africa and Asia. Proportionally the Christian church is now non-Western and its theology and mission practice are following suit.

Adapted from Andrew Walls, "The Old Age of the Missionary Movement," *IRM*, Jan. 1987

THE HISTORICAL CONTEXT OF MISSION

Christianity and Islam: The ebb and flow

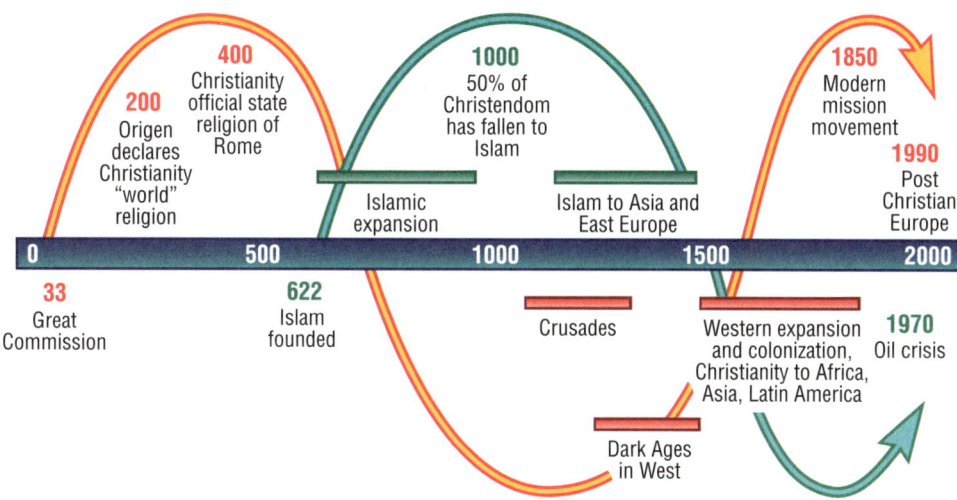

In the ebb and flow of God's history…

- By the time Islam arose in the seventh century, Christianity was a world religion and the official religion of the Roman Empire.

- Islam expanded serially from Arabia to North Africa and the Middle East, and then into the Caucasus, North Africa and Spain during seventh century.

- The classical age of Islam (A.D. 775-1300) roughly corresponded with the Dark Ages in Europe, and was the time that Islam extended its reach to Asia and central Asia.

- During the nineteenth and first half of the twentieth century, "Christian Europe" exerted colonial rule over most Muslims.

- Until the mid-1980s, there had always been more Muslims than Christians in Africa.

THE NEW CONTEXT OF WORLD MISSION

State of the World

STATE OF THE WORLD

The world by religion

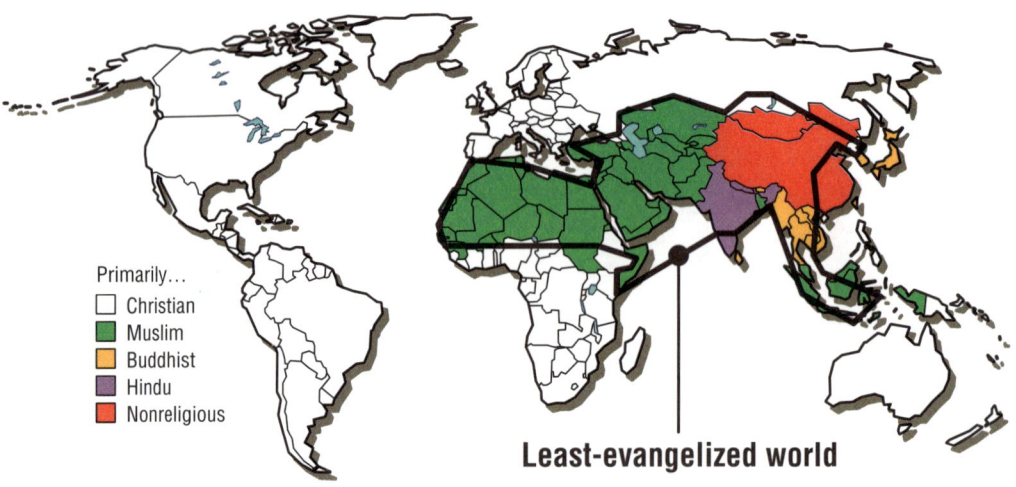

Least-evangelized world

In the year 2000…

- There will be 2.1 billion people in the world who identify themselves as members of the Christian church.

- There will be 1.2 billion Muslims. Muslims are the fastest growing major religious group, largely as a result of a high birth rate.

- There will be over one billion people who are Buddhist or who practice Chinese traditional religion.

- There will be 850 million Hindus, largely in India.

- There will be 230 million people who identify themselves as atheists.

Source: Barrett, Status of Global Mission, *IBMR*, 1996

THE NEW CONTEXT OF WORLD MISSION

STATE OF THE WORLD

The poor and the lost

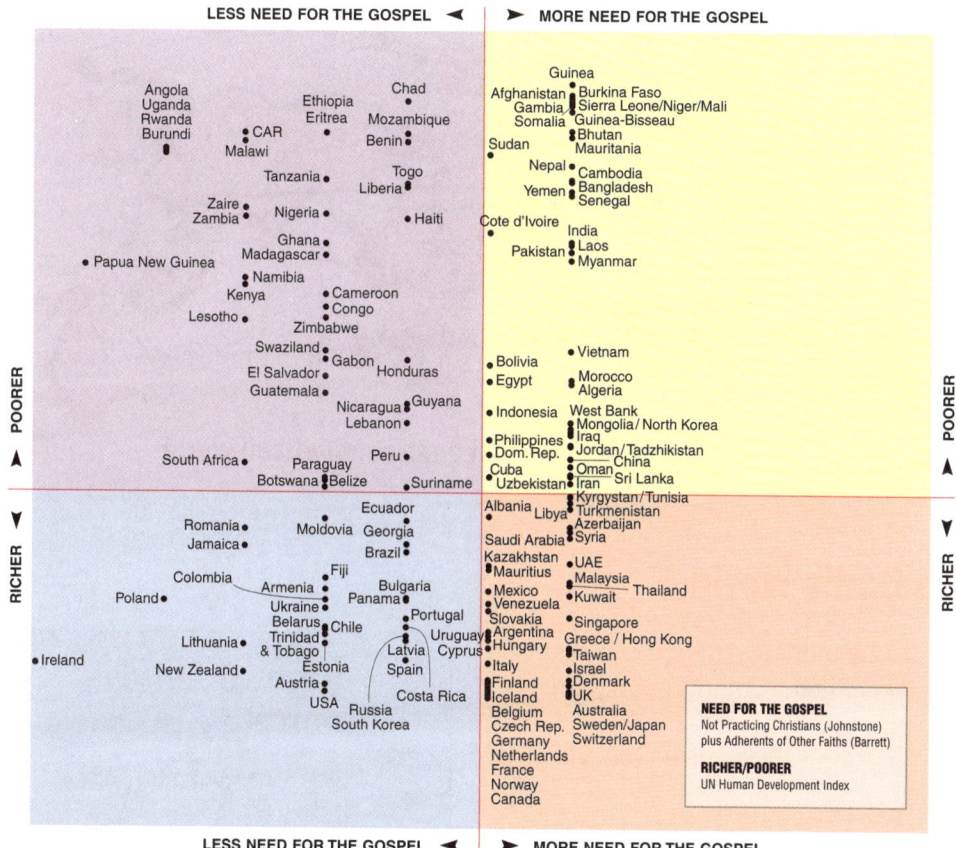

In God's world...

- A very large proportion of those who have not heard the gospel are also poor.

- Eighty-five percent of the world's poorest countries lie within the unevangelized world.

- With the demise of Marxism and communism, there is no global ideology which places the poor at the center of its vision for a better human future.

Source: Myers, *The Poor and the Lost*, 1989

STATE OF THE WORLD

How are the children?

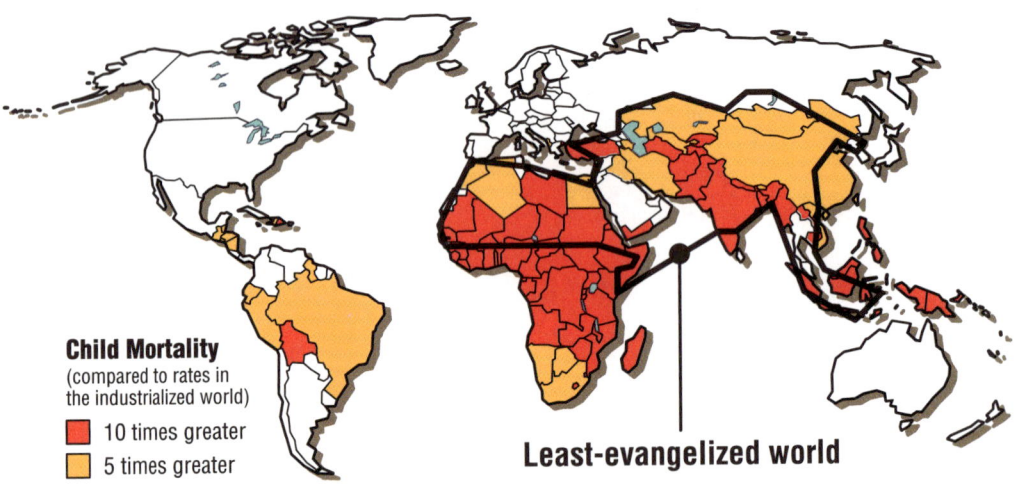

Child Mortality
(compared to rates in the industrialized world)

- 🟥 10 times greater
- 🟧 5 times greater

Least-evangelized world

In God's world...

◆ Child mortality, the average number of children per family and primary school enrollment have all improved since 1960.

◆ Yet, 15 million children die every year from preventable causes.

◆ Yet, over 350 million children will be working, instead of being in school, by the year 2000.

◆ Yet, over one million children (90% of them girls) will join the sex trade each year.

Source: "Children at Risk," 1992
The Economist, August 1996.

Highest child mortality rates

Niger
Angola
Sierra Leone
Mozambique
Afghanistan
Guinea Bissau
Guinea
Malawi
Liberia
Mali

Source: *State of the World's Children,* 1995

THE NEW CONTEXT OF WORLD MISSION

STATE OF THE WORLD

The world's poor

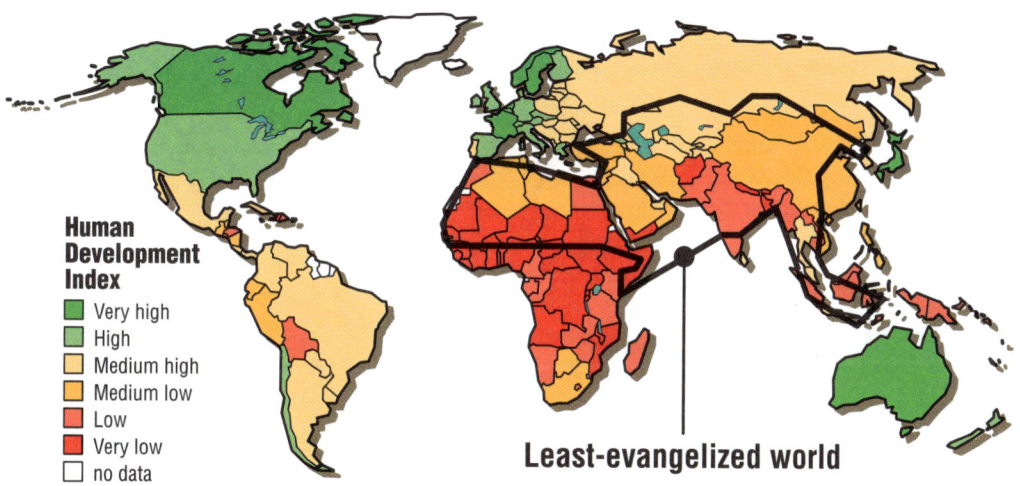

Human Development Index
- Very high
- High
- Medium high
- Medium low
- Low
- Very low
- no data

Least-evangelized world

The Human Development Index approximates knowledge (education), a long healthy life (life expectancy) and a decent standard of living (real GDP).

In God's world...

- In the last thirty years, the developing world has improved as much as the industrial world did during the whole of the nineteenth century.

- Since 1960, life expectancy in the Two-Thirds World has increased 17 years and infant mortality has dropped by more than half.

- Yet, still today one in five — one billion people — do not have access to the basic social services of health care, education, safe drinking water and adequate nutrition.

- Women are 70% of the world's poor and two-thirds of the world's illiterates.

Countries with Lowest Human Development Index

Niger	Guinea
Sierra Leone	Mozambique
Mali	Somalia
Ethiopia	Burundi
Burkina Faso	

Source: *Human Development Report 1995*

THE NEW CONTEXT OF WORLD MISSION

STATE OF THE WORLD

A world in conflict

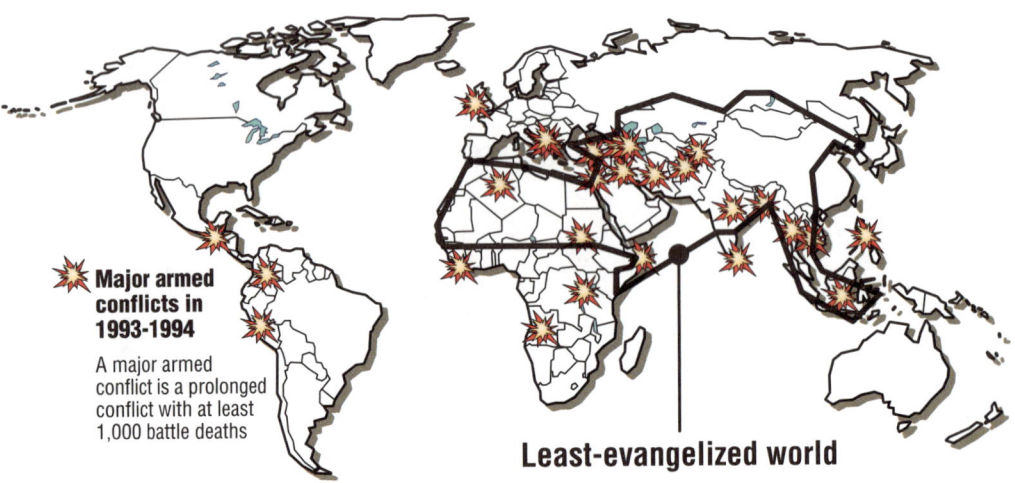

※ **Major armed conflicts in 1993-1994**

A major armed conflict is a prolonged conflict with at least 1,000 battle deaths

Least-evangelized world

In God's world...

◆ The number of ongoing wars has risen dramatically from 10 in 1960 to over 50 in 1994.

◆ Twenty-seven countries experienced major armed conflicts: Nine in Asia, six in Africa, five in Europe/Russia, four in the Middle East and three in Latin America

◆ Ninety percent of the casualties in today's armed conflicts are civilians.

Source: *State of the World Conflict Report* 1994-1995 *Human Development Report* 1995; "Complex Emergencies and the Crisis of Developmentalism"

Pollution that kills: Land mines

Egypt	23 million
Iran	16 million
Angola	15 million
Afghanistan	10 million
Cambodia	10 million
China	10 million
Iraq	10 million
Bosnia Herzegovina	3 million
Croatia	3 million
Mozambique	2 million

Source: *New York Times*, October 5, 1995

THE NEW CONTEXT OF WORLD MISSION

STATE OF THE WORLD

People without borders

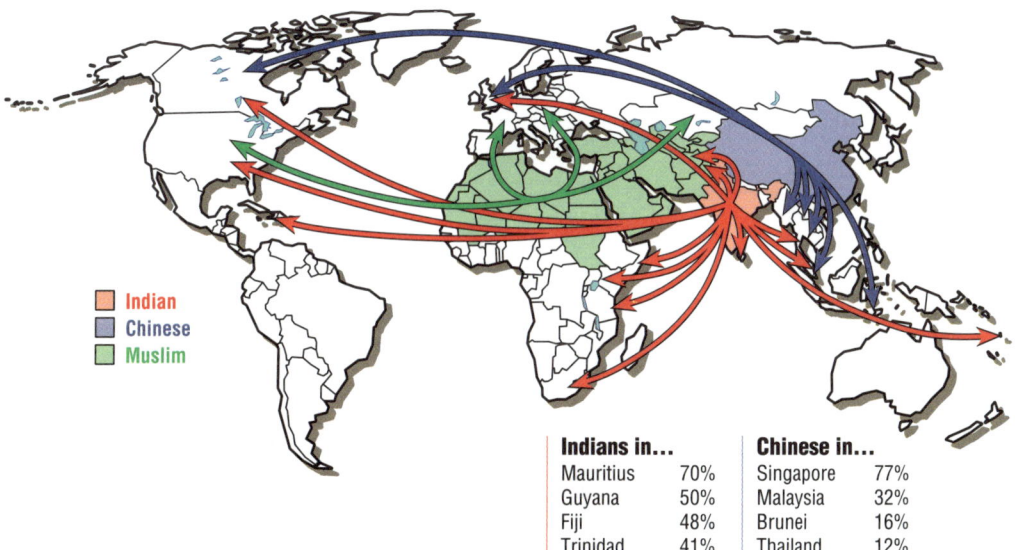

- Indian
- Chinese
- Muslim

Indians in…		Chinese in…	
Mauritius	70%	Singapore	77%
Guyana	50%	Malaysia	32%
Fiji	48%	Brunei	16%
Trinidad	41%	Thailand	12%

In these migrations…

◆ Over 55 million Chinese are living outside of mainland China.

◆ In Indonesia, the Indonesian Chinese (4%) own over 75% of the assets and 17 of the biggest 25 business groups. In Thailand, the Thai Chinese (9%) own 90% of the commercial and manufacturing assets.

◆ The primary economic unit is the extended family.

◆ Today's Muslim missionaries are students, scholars and refugees.

Source: *The Economist.* July 18, 1992

The Chinese Diaspora

Indonesia	7.2 million
Thailand	5.8 million
Malaysia	5.2 million
Singapore	2.0 million
Taiwan	1.8 million
Hong Kong	1.8 million
United States	1.8 million
Myanmar	1.5 million
Philippines	1.0 million
Vietnam	0.8 million

THE NEW CONTEXT OF WORLD MISSION

STATE OF THE WORLD

The world by population

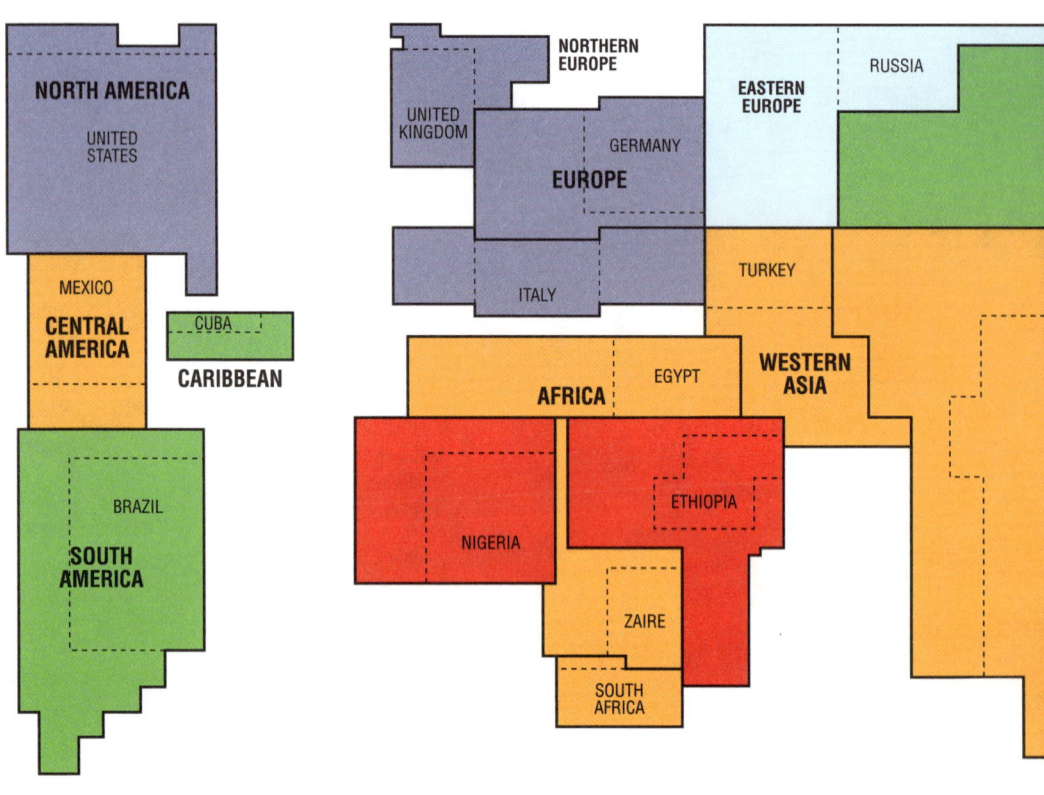

In God's world...

- The southern half of the world dwarfs the northern half.

- There are over 5.6 billion people and more on the way.

- The estimated doubling time for the poorest countries is 31 years.

- There is an explosion of the elderly. People over 80 increased from 3 million in 1900 to 53 million in 1993 and are projected at 7% of the world population by the end of the twenty-first century.

Sources: *World Population Data Sheet*, 1995 and Barrett, *AD2000 Global Monitor*, 1993

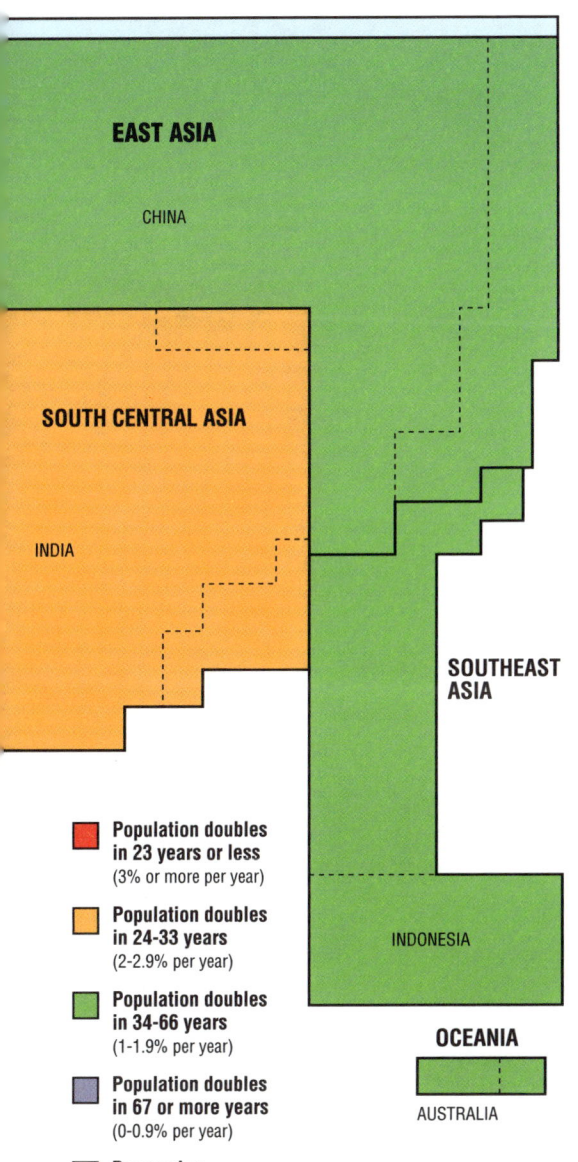

Size of Population
(country of largest population indicated in each region)

Population Doubling Time	
Fastest	
Oman	14 years
Gaza	15 years
Iraq	19 years
Maldives	19 years
Togo	19 years
Yemen	19 years
Cote d'Ivoire	20 years
Comoros	20 years
Syria	20 years
West Bank	20 years
Slowest	
Lithuania	6,931 years
Czech Republic	2,310 years
Greece	1,733 years
Slovenia	1,386 years
Sweden	990 years
Portugal	866 years
Denmark	770 years
Spain	578 years
Belgium	578 years
Austria	530 years

THE NEW CONTEXT OF WORLD MISSION

STATE OF THE WORLD

The world by income

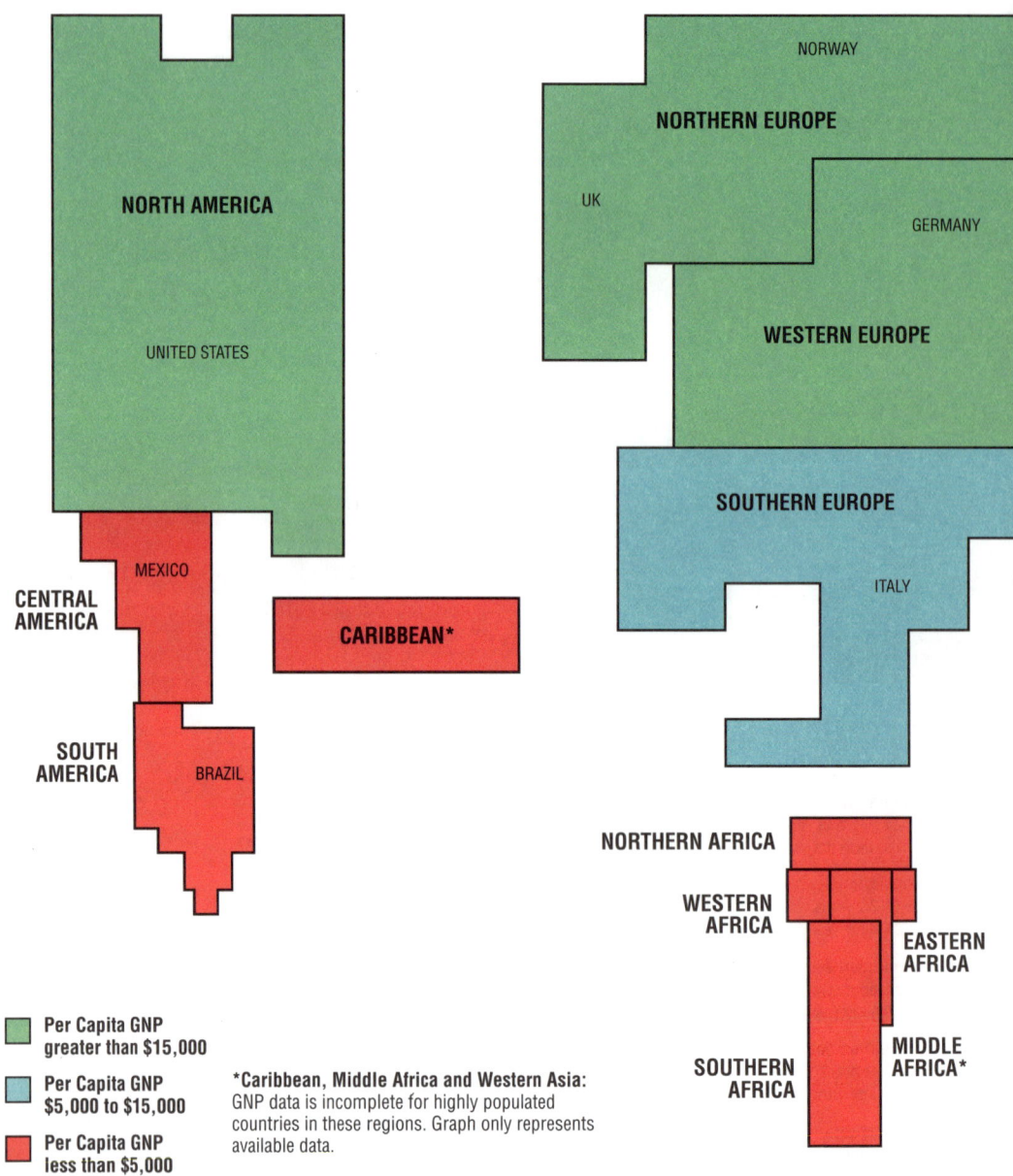

- Per Capita GNP greater than $15,000
- Per Capita GNP $5,000 to $15,000
- Per Capita GNP less than $5,000

*Caribbean, Middle Africa and Western Asia: GNP data is incomplete for highly populated countries in these regions. Graph only represents available data.

THE NEW CONTEXT OF WORLD MISSION

Per Capita Gross National Product

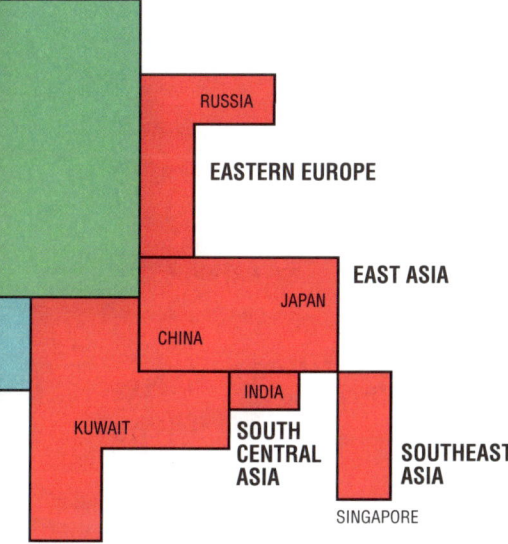

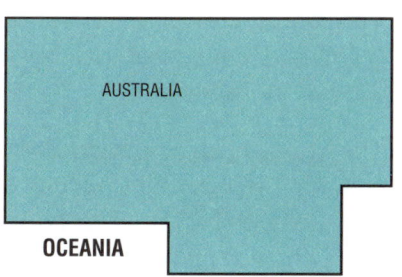

Source: World Population Data Sheet, 1995

In God's world...

◆ The northern part of the world dominates the southern part, with North America, Germany and Japan accounting for almost half of the world's income.

◆ Almost half the world's families struggle with annual incomes of less than $4,500.

◆ Of the 925 million absolute poor in the world, 211 million (or 23%) are Christians.

Sources: Barrett, *Our Globe*, 1990; *New State of the World Atlas*, 1995; World Population Data Sheet, 1995

Gross National Product
(per person)

Highest	Lowest
Switzerland	Mozambique
Luxembourg	Ethiopia
Japan	Tanzania
Denmark	Sierra Leone
Norway	Nepal
Sweden	Bangladesh
United States	Vietnam
Iceland	Burundi
Germany	Uganda
Kuwait	Rwanda
Austria	Chad

THE NEW CONTEXT OF WORLD MISSION

STATE OF THE WORLD

Global economic integration

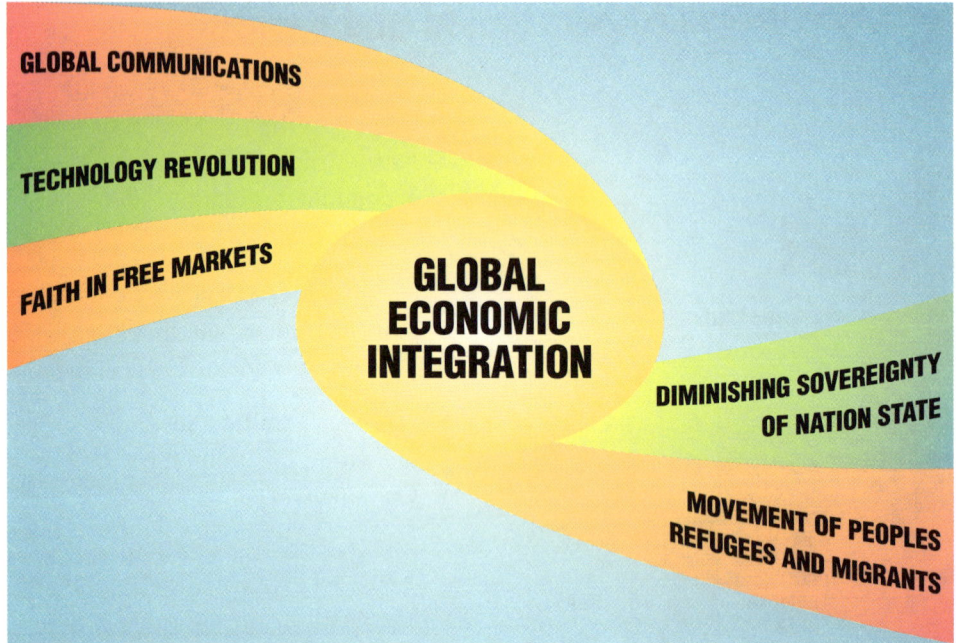

In God's world...

- The world is open for business twenty-four hours a day.

- Global communication and the computer revolution mean that nation states are losing control of their currencies, commodity prices and capital markets.

- Global economic integration is uneven, leaving some people and nations outside.

- The poorest 20% of this world only shared in 1% of global trade and 0.1% of global lending.

- The external debt of developing countries rose to $1.8 trillion in the mid-1990s and their debt service was 22% of export earnings.

Source: *Human Development Report* 1995

STATE OF THE WORLD

Global technology and communications

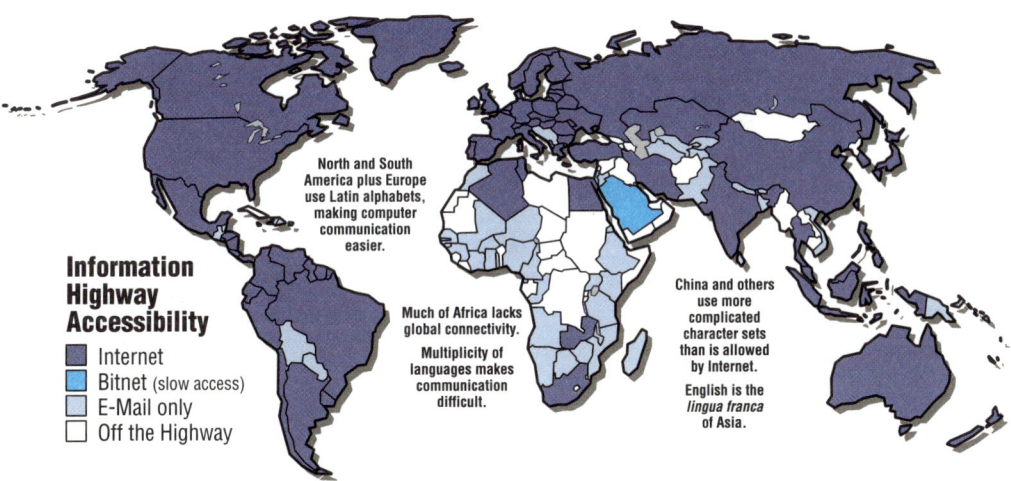

Information Highway Accessibility
- Internet
- Bitnet (slow access)
- E-Mail only
- Off the Highway

North and South America plus Europe use Latin alphabets, making computer communication easier.

Much of Africa lacks global connectivity.

Multiplicity of languages makes communication difficult.

China and others use more complicated character sets than is allowed by Internet.

English is the *lingua franca* of Asia.

In God's world...

◆ News and information is increasingly available all the time all around the world.

◆ A global youth culture — listening to the same music, seeing the same images and wearing the same shoes — is emerging, mediated by Music Television (MTV).

◆ As manipulating information becomes the engine of the global economy, the non-literate, technologically-disconnected poor may find themselves on the outside with no way in.

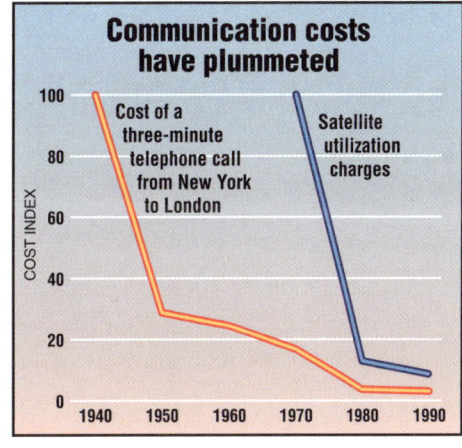

Source: *World Development Report 1995*

◆ The cost of telecommunication is increasingly independent of distance.

Sources: Pollack, *New York Times,* August 7, 1995
Cairncross, *The Economist,* September 30, 1995

THE NEW CONTEXT OF WORLD MISSION

STATE OF THE WORLD

Economic freedom

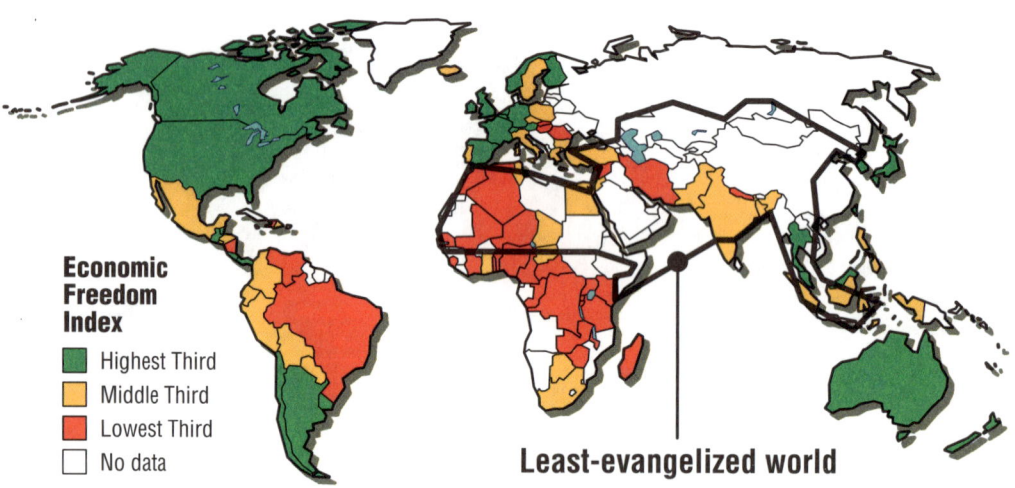

Economic Freedom Index
- Highest Third
- Middle Third
- Lowest Third
- No data

Least-evangelized world

The **Index of Economic Freedom** is comprised of measures relating to money and inflation, governments and regulations, takings and discriminatory taxation and restrictions on international exchange.

In the last 20 years...

◆ No country with consistently high economic freedom has failed to achieve a high level of income.

◆ All 17 countries where economic freedom most improved have experienced positive growth rates.

◆ Growth rates were consistently negative in countries where economic freedom declined.

◆ There is a high correlation between economic freedom and high consumption.

Source: Gwartney, Lawson and Block, *Economic Freedom of the World 1975-1995*

Economic Freedom

Highest	Lowest
Hong Kong	Zaire
New Zealand	Iran
Singapore	Algeria
United States	Syria
Switzerland	Nicaragua
United Kingdom	Brazil
Canada	Burundi
Ireland	Romania
Australia	Uganda
Japan	Zambia

THE NEW CONTEXT OF WORLD MISSION

STATE OF THE WORLD

Structures of sin

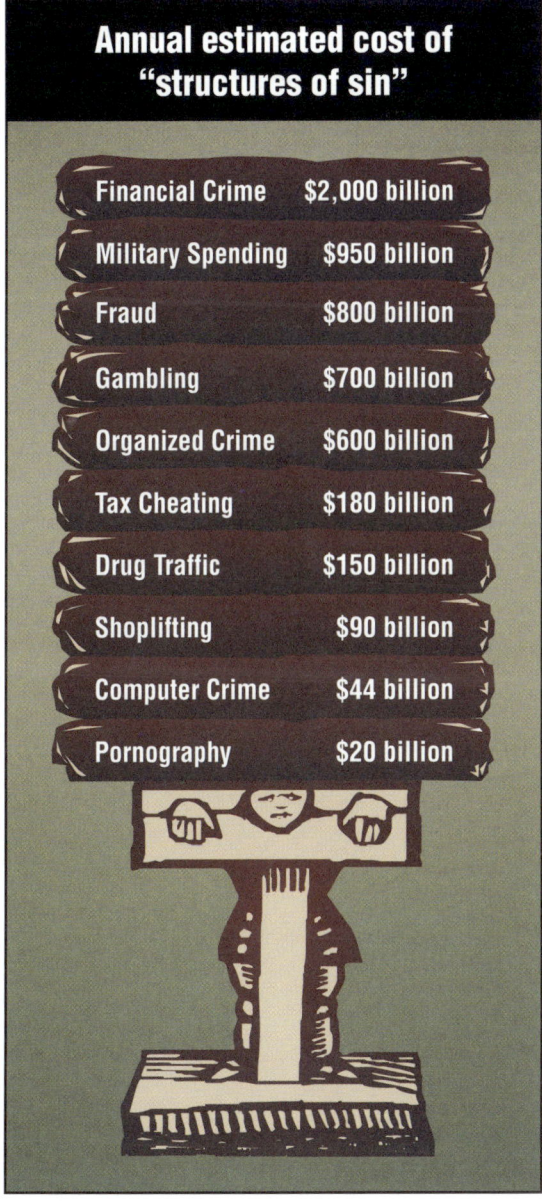

In God's world...

- Just over 30% of the gross world product is related to the "structures of sin."

- The estimated cost of the "structures of sin" every year is $5.5 trillion.

- The great majority of the activities that constitute the "structures of sin" are done by the well-off.

- The cost of extending basic social services — primary education, clean water and safe sanitation, and health care and nutrition — to people currently in absolute poverty is estimated at $34 billion.

Source: Barrett and Johnson, *Our Globe,* 1990
The Reality of Aid, 1996

STATE OF THE WORLD

The growing human family

In 2025...

- Six of every ten people in the world will live in Asia.

- Only one of every eight will live in what is now called the West.

- Even with today's accelerated mission efforts, one in fourteen — 600 million — will not have heard the gospel.

Sources: *World Population Data Sheet 1995;* Barrett, AD2025 Global Monitor, September, 1995

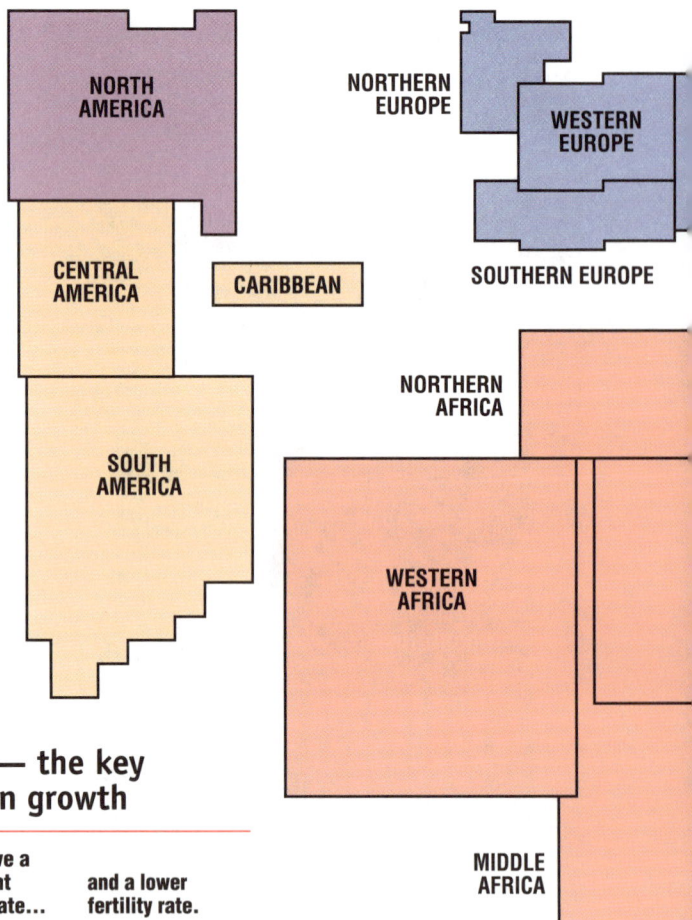

Educating women — the key to lower population growth

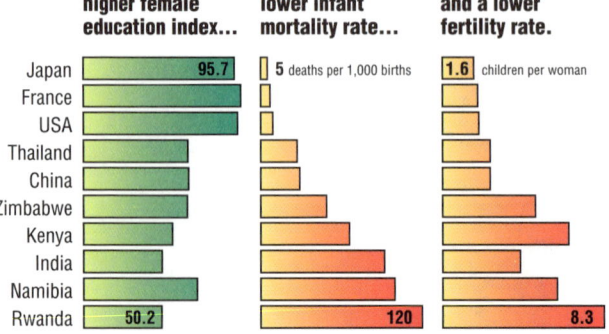

	Countries with a higher female education index...	tend to have a lower infant mortality rate...	and a lower fertility rate.
Japan	95.7	5 deaths per 1,000 births	1.6 children per woman
France			
USA			
Thailand			
China			
Zimbabwe			
Kenya			
India			
Namibia			
Rwanda	50.2	120	8.3

THE NEW CONTEXT OF WORLD MISSION

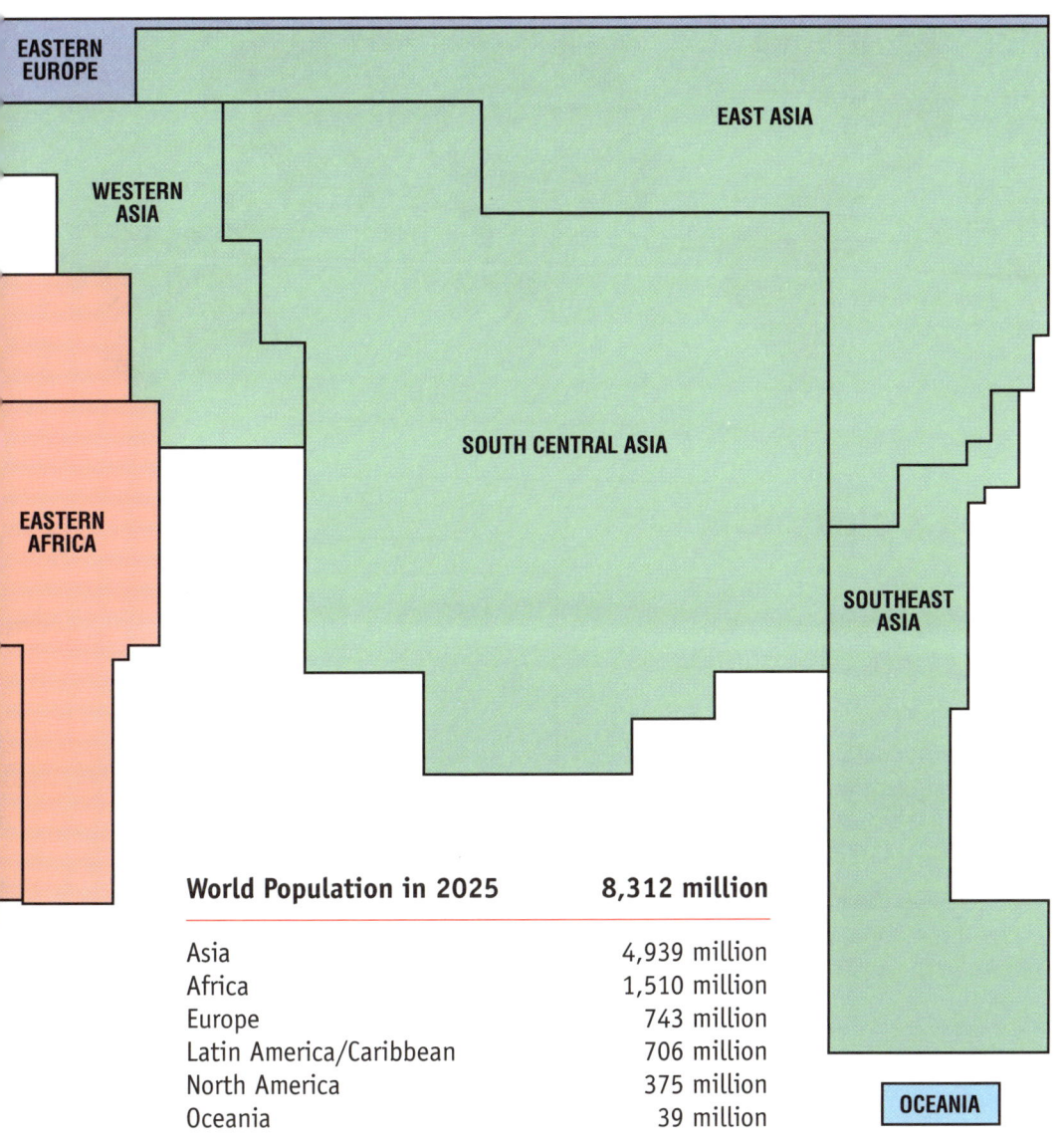

Projected Population in 2025

World Population in 2025	8,312 million
Asia	4,939 million
Africa	1,510 million
Europe	743 million
Latin America/Caribbean	706 million
North America	375 million
Oceania	39 million

STATE OF THE WORLD

Consuming the earth's resources

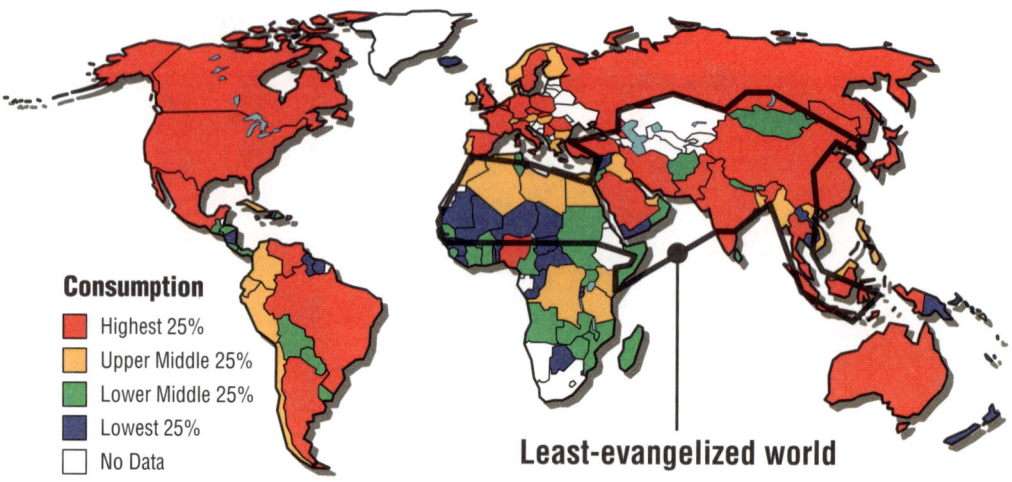

Consumption
- Highest 25%
- Upper Middle 25%
- Lower Middle 25%
- Lowest 25%
- No Data

Least-evangelized world

In God's creation...

◆ High population growth adds people where the environment is already stretched to the limit.

◆ Yet, if technology used for production and consumption are extensions of human metabolism when it comes to measuring pressure on the world's energy resources, the greatest pressure on the environment comes from the Northern and Western hemispheres.

Adapted from Mata, Onisto and Vallentyne, "Consumption: The Other Side of Population for Development," 1994

Highest Consumers

United States	22%
Former USSR	16%
China	9%
Japan	5%
India	4%
Canada	3%
Germany	3%
United Kingdom	2%
France	2%
Brazil	2%

STATE OF THE WORLD

Who has not heard?

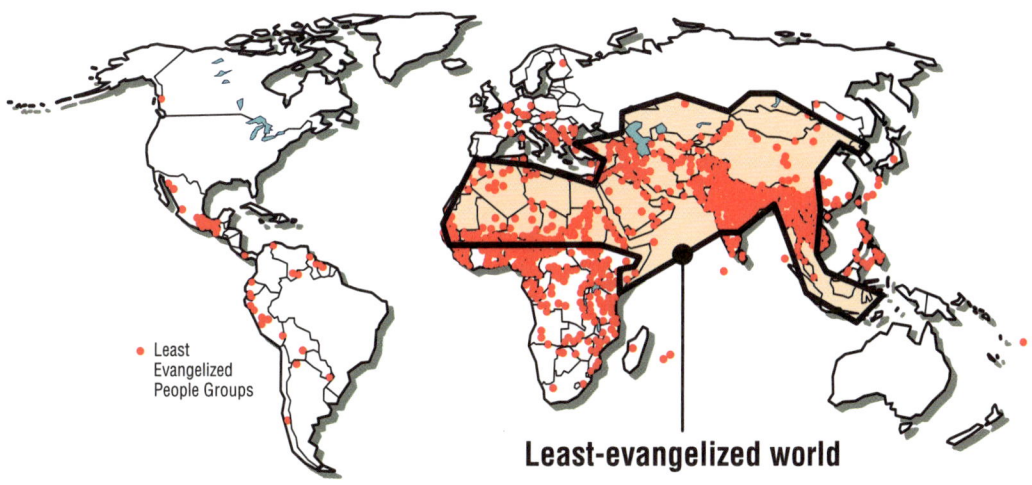

Least-evangelized world

In the least evangelized part of God's world…

- Live 86% of the people groups, of which less than 2% are Christian.
- Live over 80% of the world's poorest people.
- There are thirty-four Muslim countries, seven Buddhist nations, three Marxist nations and two Hindu countries.

Source: Barrett and Johnson, *Our Globe,* 1990

Countries with the Largest Non-Christian Populations

China
India
Indonesia
Japan
Bangladesh
Pakistan
Nigeria
Turkey
Iran

THE NEW CONTEXT OF WORLD MISSION

The Church in the World

THE CHURCH IN THE WORLD

Shape of the Christian world

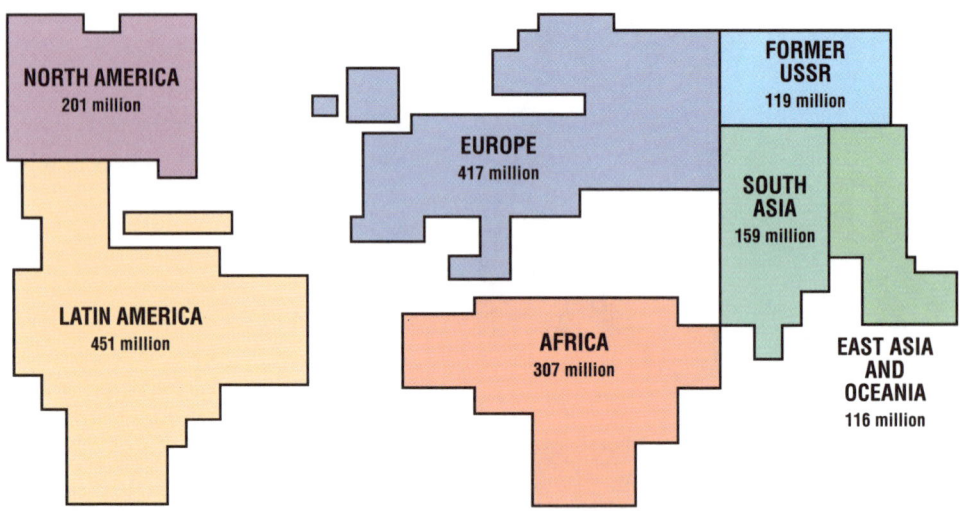

In God's world...

- Over half the Christians live in the Two-Thirds World; nearly 70% of all evangelicals live in the non-Western world.

- Over 50% of today's evangelicals are members of Pentecostal and charismatic churches.

- Two of every five professing Christians live in poor countries.

- Over half the deaths among Christians occur in poor countries.

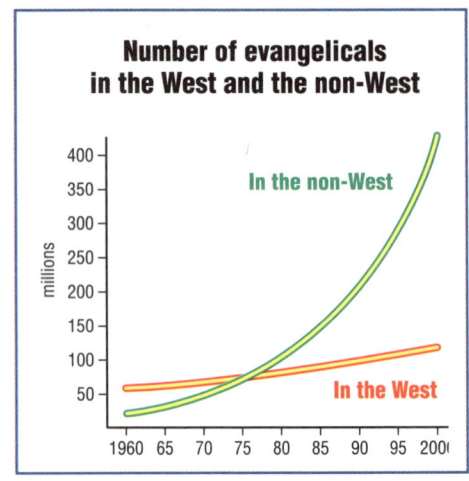

Sources: Barrett, "Annual Statistical Table on Global Mission: 1995," *IBMR*.
Johnstone, *Operation World*, 1993.

THE CHURCH IN THE WORLD

State of the Christian church

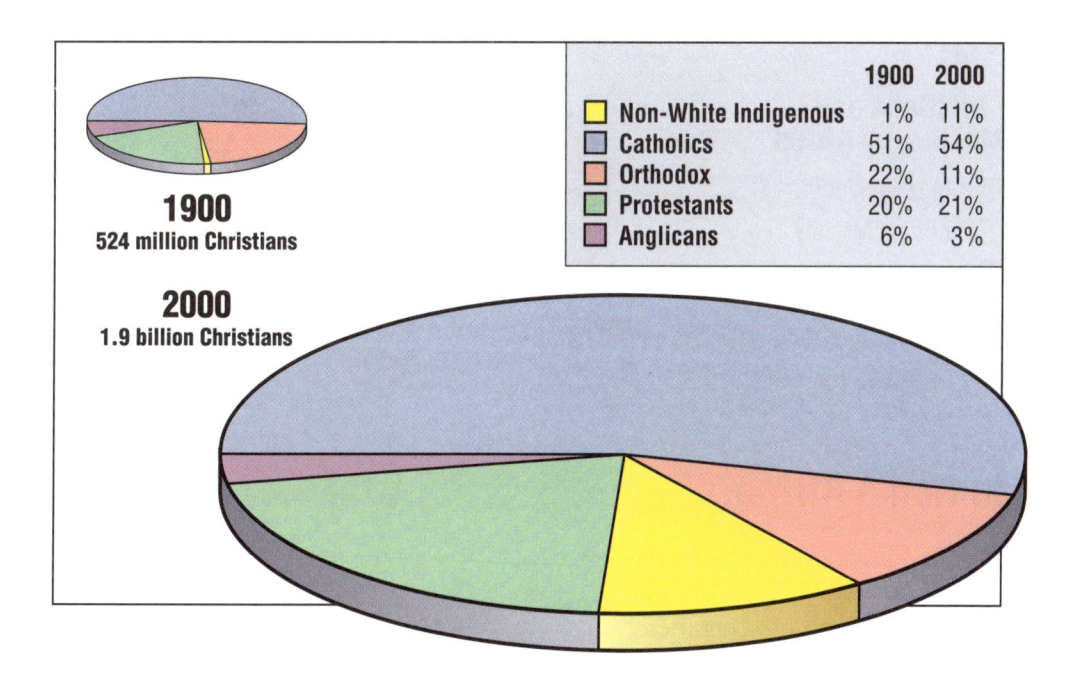

	1900	2000
Non-White Indigenous	1%	11%
Catholics	51%	54%
Orthodox	22%	11%
Protestants	20%	21%
Anglicans	6%	3%

1900
524 million Christians

2000
1.9 billion Christians

During this century in the body of Christ...

- The percentage of Christians active in some form of mission today is at an all-time high of 36%.

- The non-white indigenous church increased eleven-fold to 11% of all Christians today.

- A little over 26% of all Christians are Pentecostals or charismatics. Pentecostals and charismatics increased 130-fold from 3.7 million in 1900 to 480 million today.

- The proportion of Roman Catholics among Christians increased to 54%, up from 51% in 1990.

- The proportion of Protestants remained unchanged. The proportion of Orthodox and Anglicans declined by half to 11% and 3%, respectively.

Source: Barrett, "Status of Global Mission 1996," *IBMR*.

THE NEW CONTEXT OF WORLD MISSION

The church in Africa

Christians and Muslims in Africa

- ◼ Christian Minority
- ◼ Christian Majority
- ◼ Muslim Majority
- ◼ Areas of Tension

In God's Africa...

◆ The Christian church first took root in North Africa in the second through the fourth centuries.

◆ There were more Muslims than Christians in Africa until the mid-1980s.

◆ Africa is experiencing the fastest church growth of any region.

◆ One third of this region's population does not get enough to eat.

◆ The theological and ministry focus in Africa is on traditional religions and extending the rule of God to ethnic, economic and political life.

Source: Walls, "Significance of Christianity in Africa" *Human Development Report 1995*

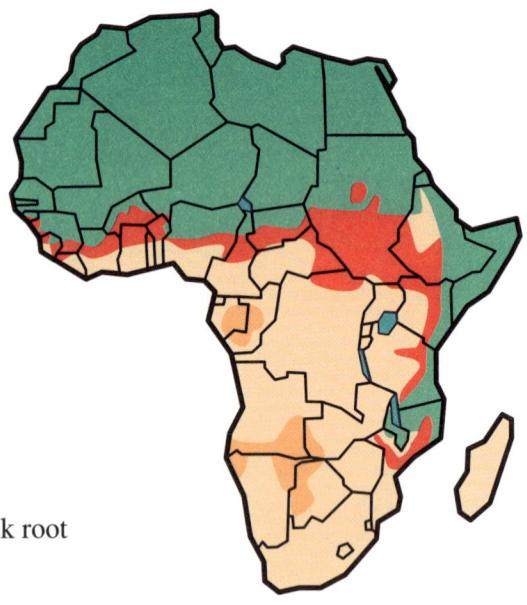

The Largest Christian Majorities
(among larger countries)

Zaire	92%
Gabon	82%
Lesotho	77%
Congo	76%
Rwanda	76%
Burundi	75%
South Africa	72%
Swaziland	70%
Kenya	70%
Angola	69%

Source: *Operation World*, 1993

THE CHURCH IN THE WORLD

The church in Asia

Christians in Asia
- 0% – 2%
- 2% – 5%
- 5% – 10%
- Over 10%

In God's Asia…

◆ The Christian church went to Asia in the second century from the Church of the East in Syria, and again to Asia in the 16th century from Spain and Portugal.

◆ Asian Christians have faced the church's greatest persecutions. Religious discrimination directed toward Christians is once again on the rise.

◆ The theological focus is on uniqueness of Christ in the context of the major world religions. The ministry focus is on Christian witness.

◆ The largest Christian populations are found in the Philippines and China (61 million each), India (33 million) and Indonesia (25 million).

Sources: Moffat, *The History of Christianity in Asia*, 1992; *Operation World*, 1995

The Largest Christian Minorities
(among larger countries)

South Korea	35%
Hong Kong	14%
Indonesia	13%
Singapore	12%
Vietnam	9%
Sri Lanka	8%
Malaysia	7%
Myanmar	6%
People's Republic of China	5%

Source: *Operation World*, 1993

THE NEW CONTEXT OF WORLD MISSION

THE CHURCH IN THE WORLD

The church in Europe

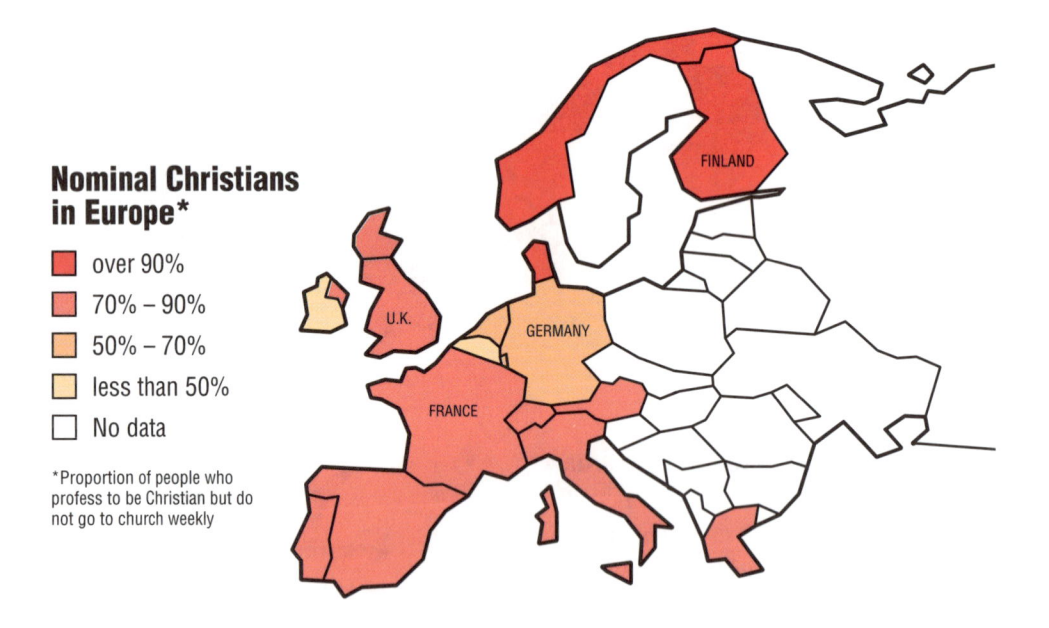

Nominal Christians in Europe*

- ■ over 90%
- ■ 70% – 90%
- ■ 50% – 70%
- ■ less than 50%
- □ No data

*Proportion of people who profess to be Christian but do not go to church weekly

In God's Europe…

- ◆ The most religious countries in Europe are Ireland and Poland.

- ◆ Europe has more nominal Christians than the rest of the world put together.

- ◆ Animism in the form of magic continues to thrive. The outcome of the conflict between Christianity and modernity may not be secularism, but animism.

Source: Greeley, "Religion Around the World," 1992. Brierley, *UK Christian Handbook 1992-93.*

Magic Index
Proportion who indicate high belief in faith healers, astrology, good luck charms and fortune tellers.

Slovenia	60%
Britain	42%
West Germany	38%
Northern Ireland	37%
Ireland	34%
East Germany	32%

THE NEW CONTEXT OF WORLD MISSION

THE CHURCH IN THE WORLD

The church in Latin America

Protestants in Latin America

- ■ over 20%
- ■ 10% – 20%
- ■ 5% –10%
- ■ less than 5%
- □ no data

In God's Latin America...

◆ The Christian church came 450 years ago from Spain and Portugal.

◆ The rapid rise of Pentecostal and charismatic churches among the poor and now the middle class is one of the startling new missiological facts of this century.

◆ The largest population of Protestants is in Brazil (32 million).

◆ The income share of the richest 20% is fifteen times that of the poorest 20% in many countries.

◆ The theological and ministry focus is on the struggle to be with and for the poor.

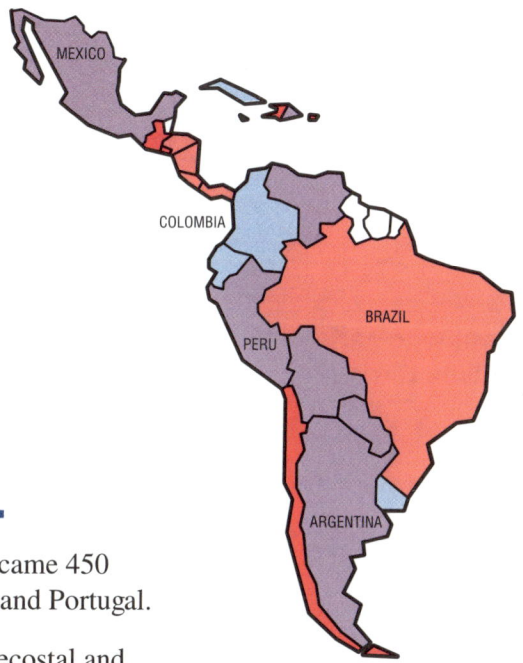

Source: *Human Development Report* 1995
Operation World, 1995
THE NEW CONTEXT OF WORLD MISSION

The Largest Protestant Minorities

Chile	28%
Guatemala	24%
El Salvador	20%
Brazil	19%
Nicaragua	18%
Panama	17%
Honduras	11%
Costa Rica	11%
Bolivia	9%
Argentina	8%

Source: *Operation World*, 1993

THE CHURCH IN THE WORLD

The status of the Great Commission

Have heard, limited response

Least-evangelized world

Those who call themselves Christians

In the last years of this century...

- The percentage of Christians in the world has remained virtually unchanged at 34% since 1900. This has obscured an important sea change.

- Since 1975, evangelization has outstripped the increase in non-Christians for the first time in modern mission history.

- By the year 2000, one billion people will still have never heard the gospel, but the trend in the number of unevangelized will be decreasing.

Source: Barrett and Johnson, *AD2000 Monitor*, April and July 1994.

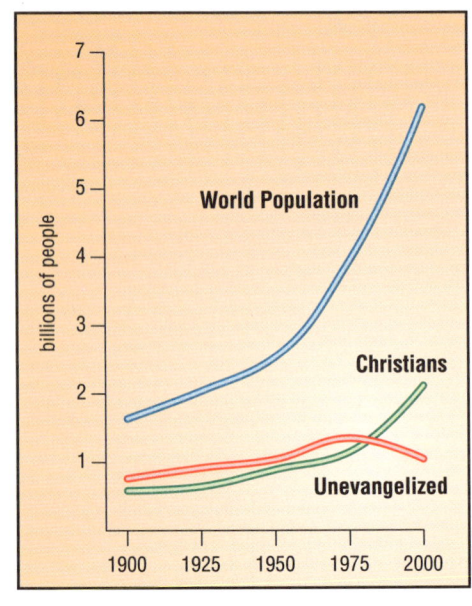

Source: *Operation World*, 1993

THE NEW CONTEXT OF WORLD MISSION

Challenges to Christian Mission

CHALLENGES TO CHRISTIAN MISSION

Who needs to hear?

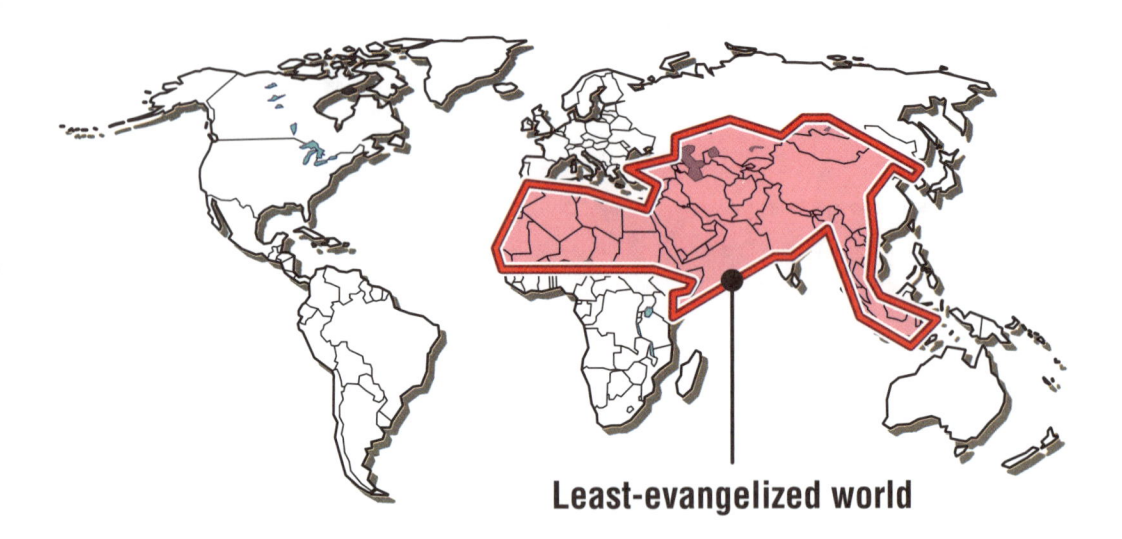

Least-evangelized world

In the least evangelized part of God's world...

- Over 1.1 billion people live who have little chance to hear the gospel unless someone goes to tell them.

- There are 500 people groups who have never heard the Good News.

- The church is deploying only 4,000 of its 332,000 missionaries.

Source: Barrett and Johnson, *AD2000 Global Monitor*, October 1994

Largest Least Evangelized

Bengali (Bangladesh)	120 million
Han groups (China)	97 million
Bhojpuri Bihari (India)	62 million
Punjabi (Pakistan)	57 million
Awadi (India)	53 million
Turks (Turkey)	42 million
Urdu (India)	36 million
Orisi (India)	33 million
Maitili (India)	30 million
Burmese (Myanmar)	29 million

Source: Barrett and Johnson, *AD2000 Monitor*, January 1994

CHALLENGES TO CHRISTIAN MISSION

Children and youth

Children and youth as percent of population
- Very low (15%-25%)
- Low (26%-36%)
- Moderate (37%-41%)
- High (42%-46%)
- Very high (47%-51%)

Least-evangelized world

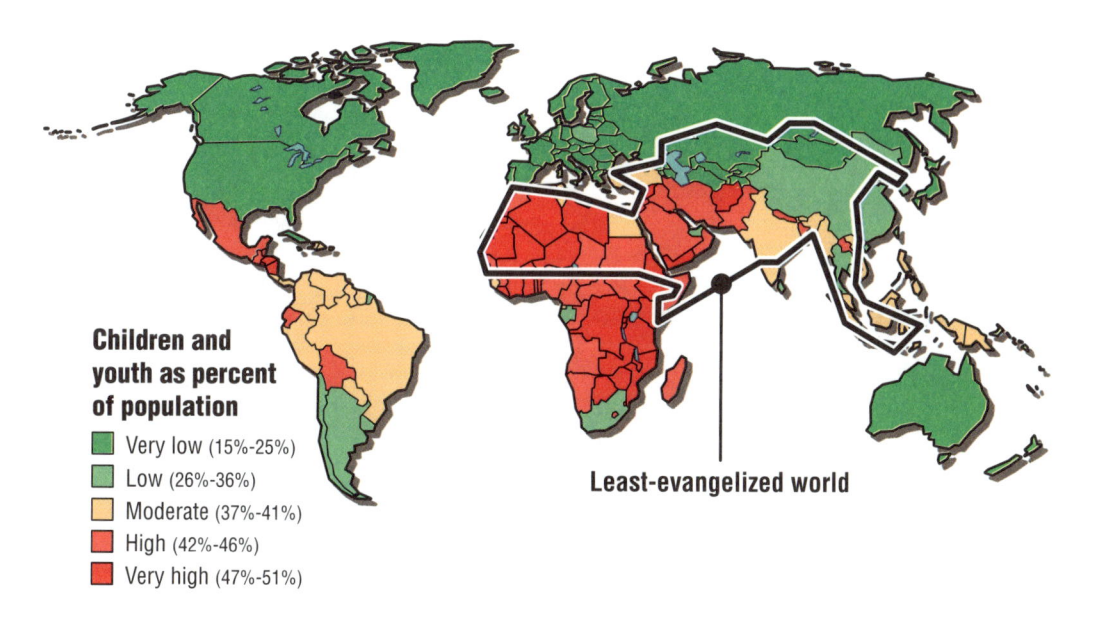

In God's world…

- One-third of the world's population is under the age of 15, and 85% of these children and youth live in the Two-Thirds World.

- The great majority of people make life-shaping faith decisions before they reach the age of 20.

- MARC estimates that over 80% of the world's young people — 1.4 billion — are growing up in non-Christian settings or non-Christian homes.

Source: Myers, "State of the World's Children," *IBMR*, 1993

Highest number of children under the age of 15

China
India
Indonesia
United States
Pakistan
Brazil
Bangladesh
Russia
Mexico

Source: *World Population Data Sheet*, 1994

CHALLENGES TO CHRISTIAN MISSION

The growing cities in the south

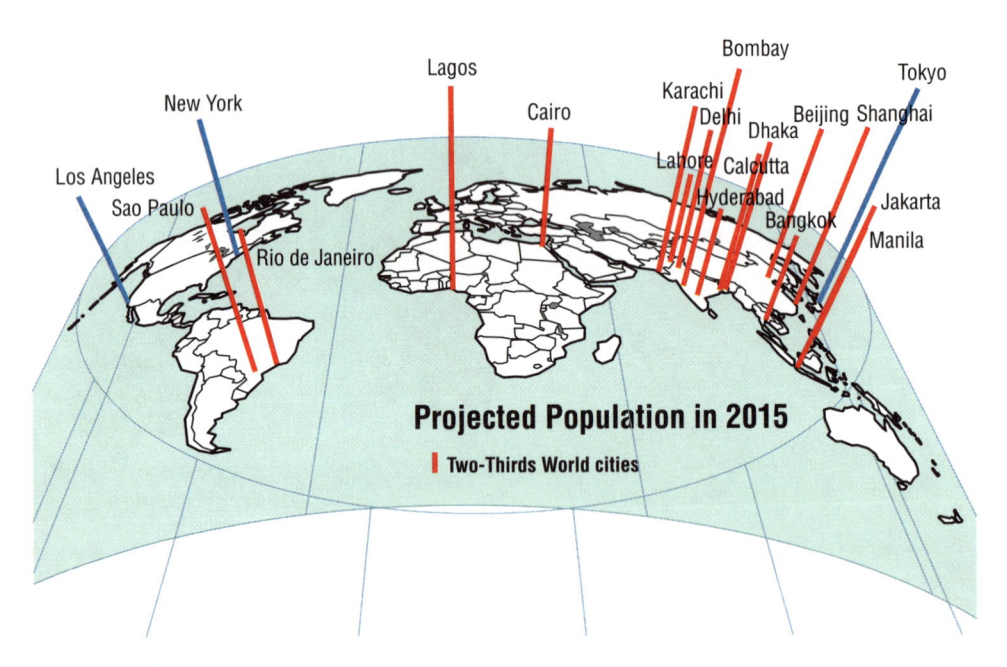

Projected Population in 2015
- Two-Thirds World cities

Cities labeled: Los Angeles, New York, Sao Paulo, Rio de Janeiro, Lagos, Cairo, Karachi, Lahore, Delhi, Bombay, Hyderabad, Calcutta, Dhaka, Bangkok, Beijing, Shanghai, Tokyo, Jakarta, Manila

In God's world...

◆ By 2025, more than one-quarter of the world's population will be poor and living in the squatter settlements of the Two-Thirds World.

◆ 62% of all Christians—over one billion people—live in urban settings.

◆ There are more than 100 million street children in today's world class cities—25% of whom both work and sleep in the streets.

◆ By 2015, seventeen of the twenty-one cities with a population of over 10 million will be in the Two-Thirds World.

Sources: Barrett, "Status of Global Mission 1996," *IBMR*; Linthicum, *Empowering the Poor*

THE NEW CONTEXT OF WORLD MISSION

CHALLENGES TO CHRISTIAN MISSION

The Muslim world

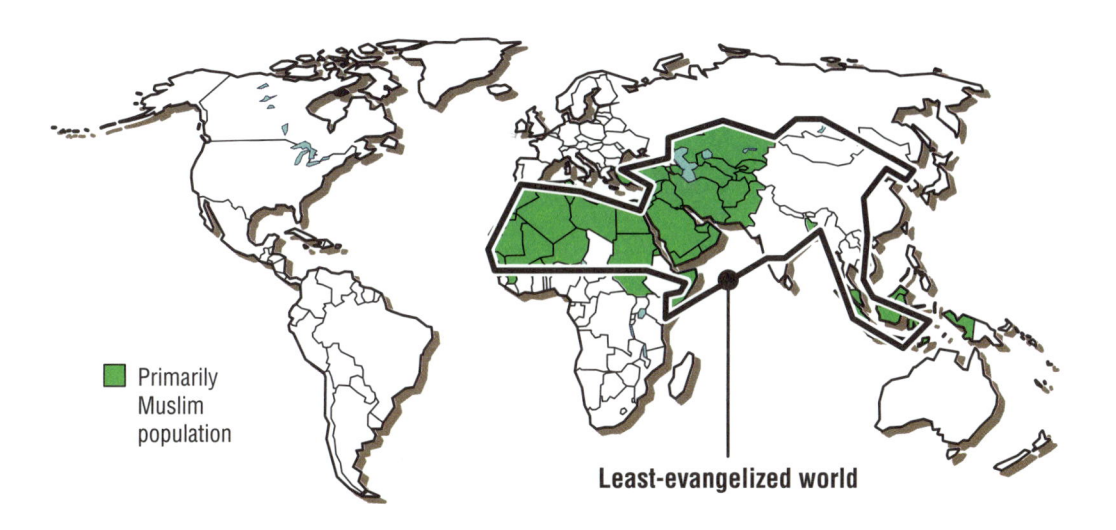

■ Primarily Muslim population

Least-evangelized world

In God's world...

◆ Over 1.1 billion people in the world are Muslim.

◆ Islam is one of the fastest growing major religious groups, largely as a result of population growth in Asia and Africa.

◆ The majority of Muslims live in South Asia, not the Middle East.

◆ Over 80% of all Muslims have never heard the gospel, yet regard Jesus as a key prophet.

Source: Barrett, "Status of Global Mission 1996," IBMR

Countries with largest Muslim populations

Indonesia
Pakistan
India
Bangladesh
Turkey
Iran
Egypt
Nigeria
China
Morocco
Algeria
Uzbekistan

Source: Zwemer Institute, 1992

THE NEW CONTEXT OF WORLD MISSION

CHALLENGES TO CHRISTIAN MISSION

Allocating our resources for mission

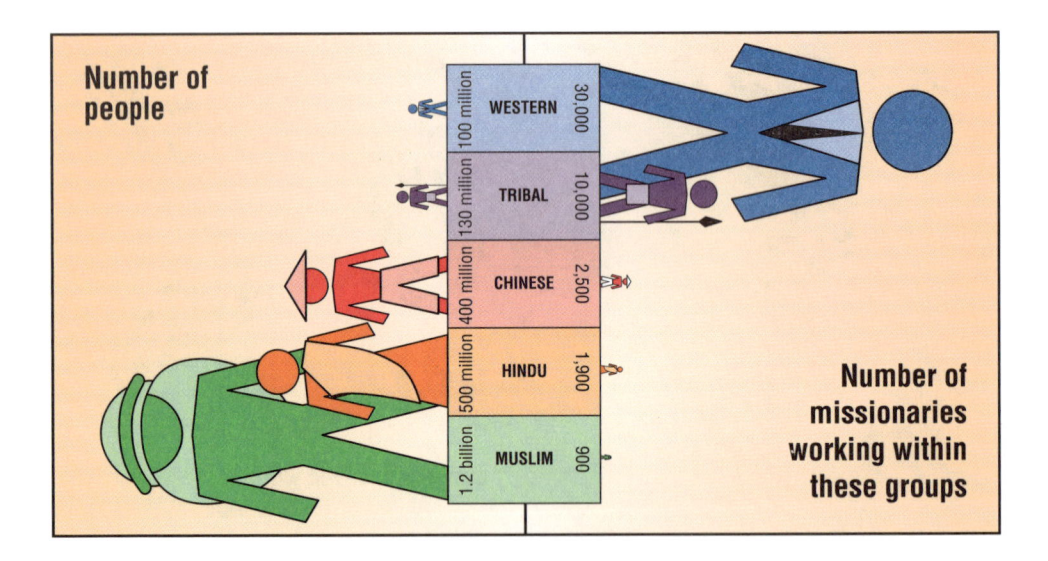

Number of people		Number of missionaries working within these groups
100 million	WESTERN	30,000
130 million	TRIBAL	10,000
400 million	CHINESE	2,500
500 million	HINDU	1,900
1.2 billion	MUSLIM	900

In the unevangelized part of God's world...

◆ Christians are allocating only 1.2% of their mission funding and their foreign missionaries to the 1.1 billion people who live in the unevangelized world.

◆ Only 1% of the Scripture distribution and only 3% of the languages for which the Bible has been translated are directed toward the least evangelized world.

Source: Barrett and Johnson, *AD2000 Global Monitor*, October 1994.

Protestant Missionaries Working in Another Culture

United States	64,378
Asia	23,681
Europe	19,564
Africa	12,829
International	6,457
Pacific	6,211
Latin America	4,482
Other	890
Total	138,492

Source: *Operation World*, 1993

CHALLENGES TO CHRISTIAN MISSION

The sinned-against

The sinned-against have no names or faces to most of us.

In God's world...

- Over 1.1 billion people live on less than one dollar (US) a day.

- Every day, 25,000 people — most of them children — die from the results of dirty drinking water.

- One out of four human beings do not have access to any form of health care.

- There are 47 million refugees and displaced people.

- Half the world's people are unable to vote.

- Over 3 billion people are denied the freedom to teach ideas.

Sources: Barrett and Johnson, *Our Globe*, 1990; *World Development Report 1995*

CHALLENGES TO CHRISTIAN MISSION

Complex humanitarian emergencies & refugees

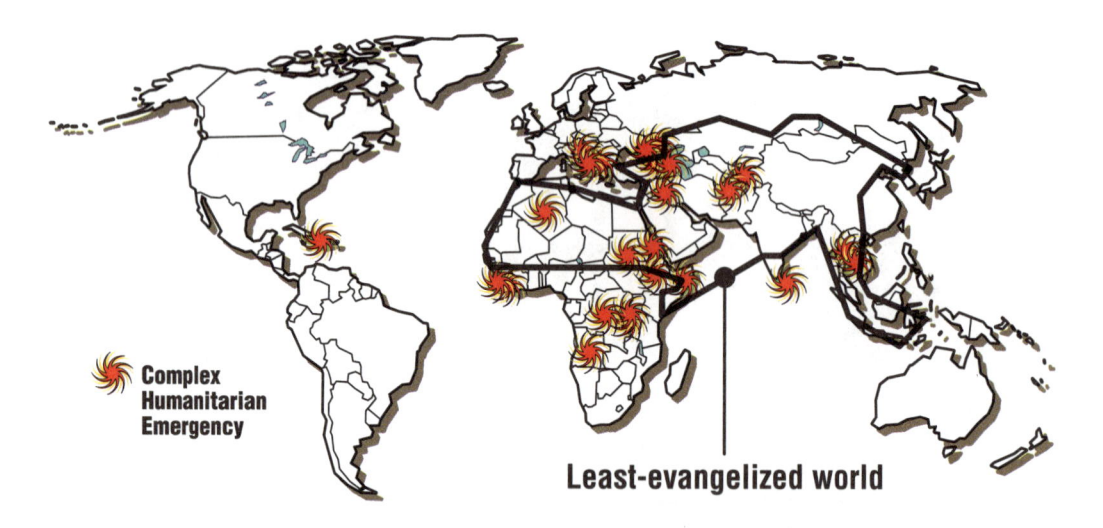

🌀 **Complex Humanitarian Emergency**

Least-evangelized world

A **Complex Humanitarian Emergency** combines internal conflict, large-scale displacement of people, mass famine and fragile or failing economic, political and social institutions

In God's world...

◆ Complex humanitarian emergencies are a relatively new phenomenon. The number of complex humanitarian emergencies has increased from an average of five a year in the early 1980s to 14 in 1984 and 21 in 1994.

◆ The number of refugees has exploded from 3 million in 1970 to 23 million in 1994. Another 27 million are displaced within their own countries.

◆ Over two-thirds of the world's refugees are Muslims.

Source: *State of the World's Refugees 1995*
Medecins sans Frontieres, 1992.
World Refugee Survey, 1995

Largest CHEs and Population at Risk

Ethiopia	4.3 million
Afghanistan	4.2 million
Rwanda	4.0 million
Angola	3.7 million
Sudan	3.0 million
Bosnia	2.5 million
Liberia	2.1 million
Eritrea	1.6 million
Somalia	1.1 million
Haiti	1.3 million

Source: *Hunger 1996*

THE NEW CONTEXT OF WORLD MISSION

CHALLENGES TO CHRISTIAN MISSION

The crucial importance of women

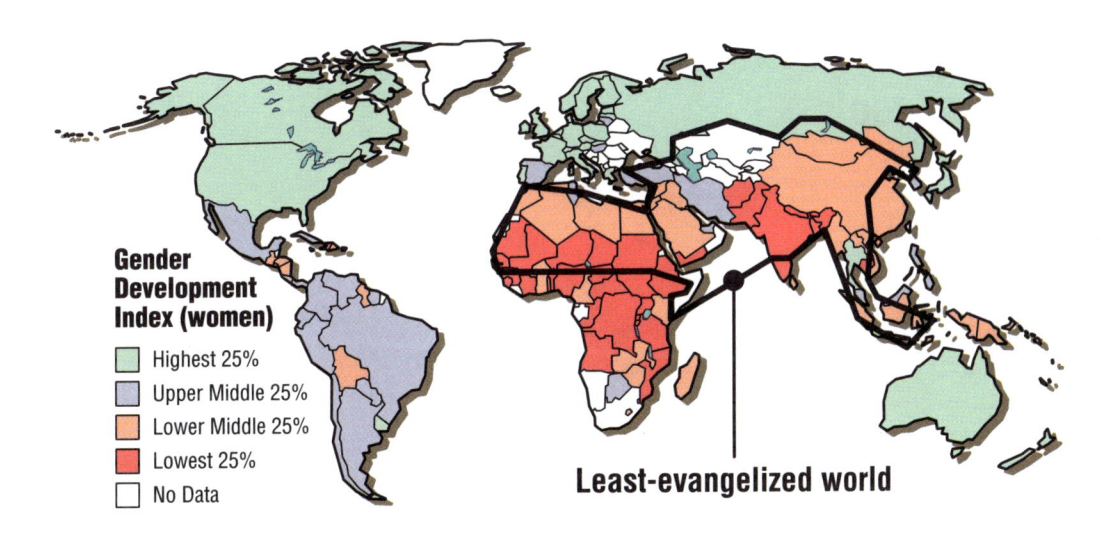

Gender Development Index (women)
- Highest 25%
- Upper Middle 25%
- Lower Middle 25%
- Lowest 25%
- No Data

Least-evangelized world

In God's world...

◆ There is a very high correlation between female literacy and positive changes in under-five mortality, fertility rates and economic development.

◆ Yet, the world average for female children reaching the fifth grade is only 68%.

◆ Yet, the proportion of women in all levels of schooling in the Two-Thirds World is only 29%. In the West it is 81%.

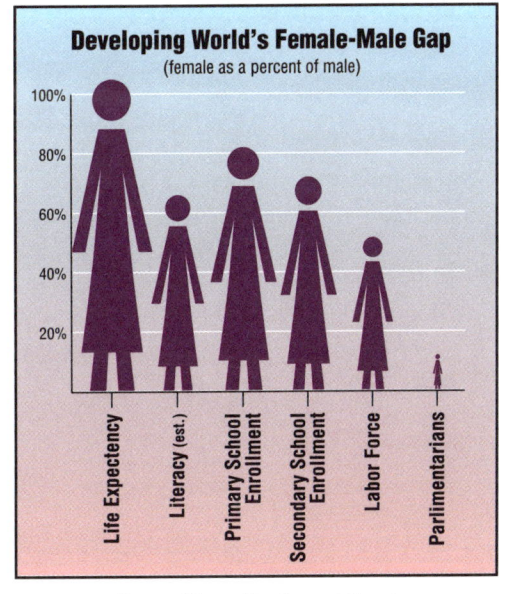

Source: *Human Development Report 1995*

Developing World's Female-Male Gap
(female as a percent of male)

- Life Expectancy
- Literacy (est.)
- Primary School Enrollment
- Secondary School Enrollment
- Labor Force
- Parliamentarians

Source: *Human Development Report*

THE NEW CONTEXT OF WORLD MISSION

CHALLENGES TO CHRISTIAN MISSION

Promoting equitable human development

Among God's people everywhere...

- More than three-fourths of the world's people live in developing countries. The richest 20% of the world enjoy 85% of the global income.

- In Asia's high growth economies, the incomes of workers and peasants has grown faster than executives or entrepreneurs.

- Recent economic studies suggest that greater income equality is compatible with faster growth.

- In less equal societies, concerns for social and political conflict are more likely to lead to government policies which hinder growth.

Sources: *Human Development Report 1995;* Nasar, *New York Times,* January 5, 1995; Persson and Tabellini, *American Economic Review,* 1994.

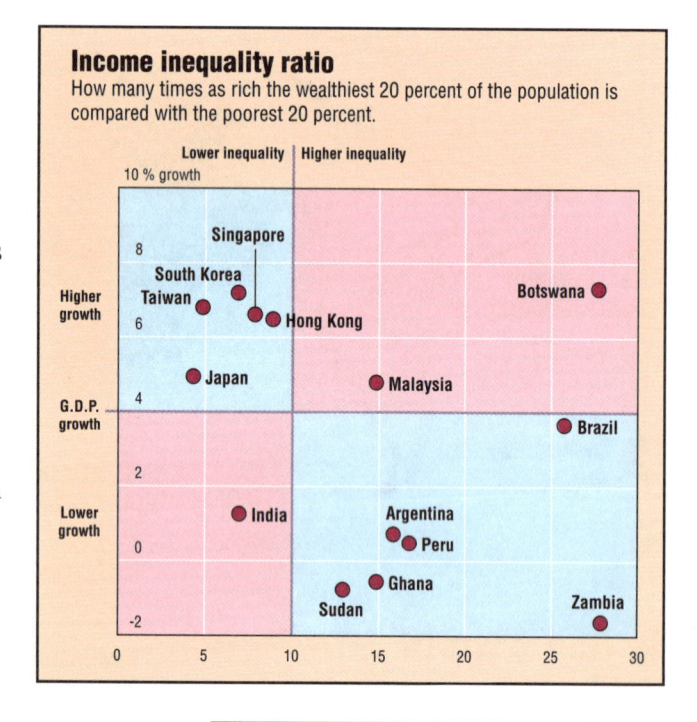

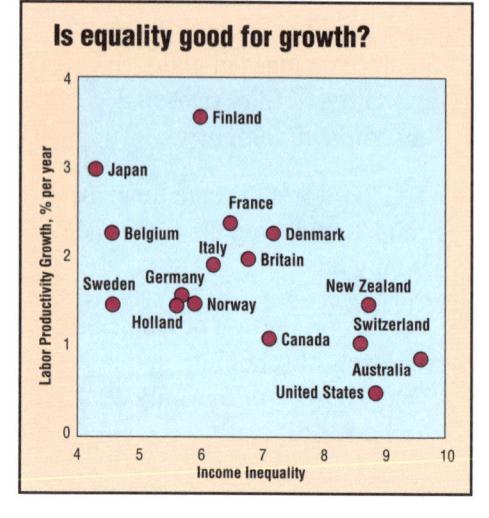

Income inequality ratio
How many times as rich the wealthiest 20 percent of the population is compared with the poorest 20 percent.

Is equality good for growth?

52   THE NEW CONTEXT OF WORLD MISSION

CHALLENGES TO CHRISTIAN MISSION

Caring for creation

The connections between poverty, population and the environment

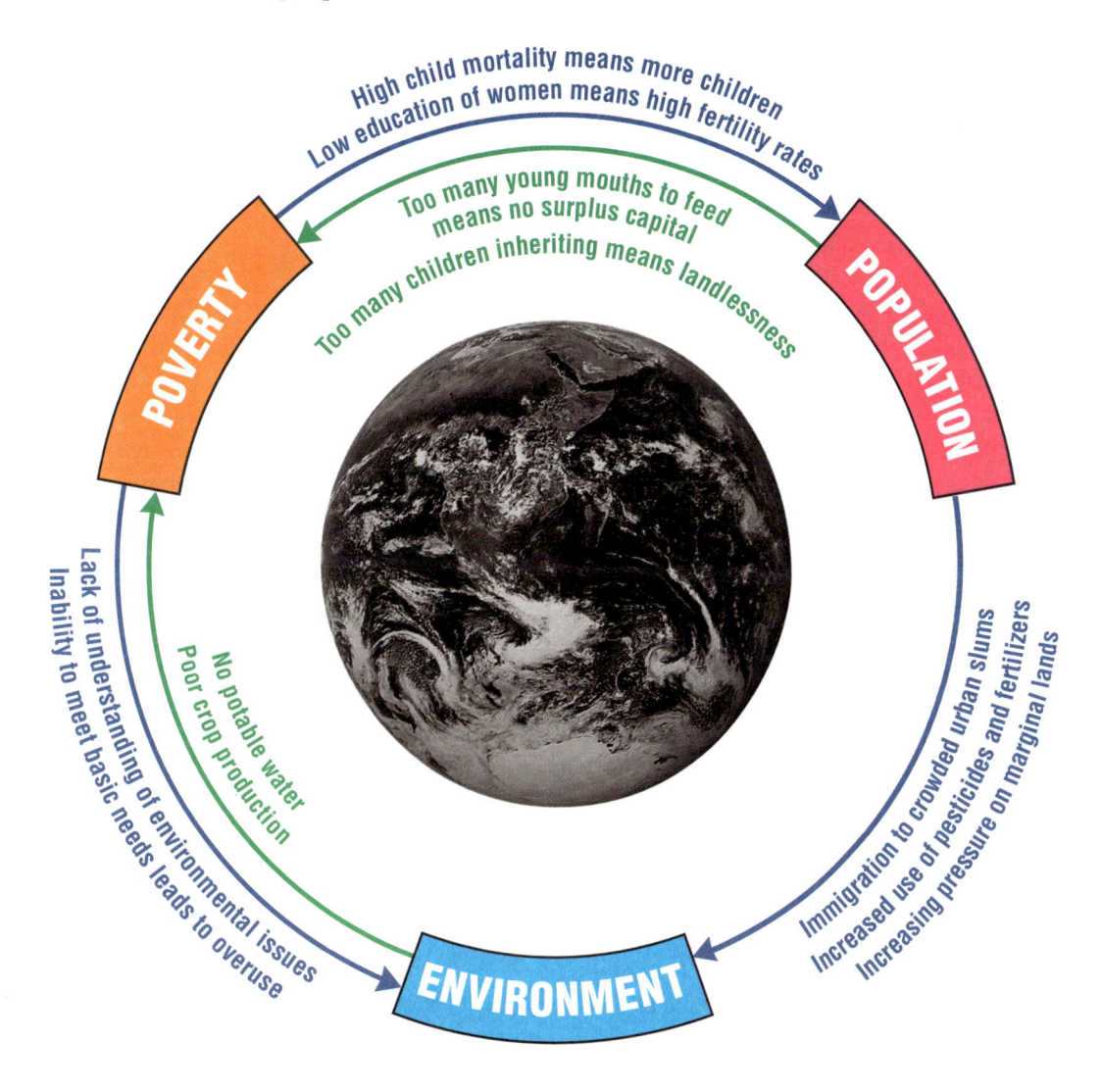

- High child mortality means more children
- Low education of women means high fertility rates
- Too many young mouths to feed means no surplus capital
- Too many children inheriting means landlessness

POVERTY → **POPULATION**

- Immigration to crowded urban slums
- Increased use of pesticides and fertilizers
- Increasing pressure on marginal lands

- Lack of understanding of environmental issues
- Inability to meet basic needs leads to overuse
- No potable water
- Poor crop production

ENVIRONMENT

THE NEW CONTEXT OF WORLD MISSION

53

Conclusions

Declaring a whole gospel

People are whole beings — body, mind and soul, intertwined in a seamless way. People are not disembodied souls nor spiritless bodies. Furthermore, they live in communities that are physical, social and spiritual.

The pain of this world is the same. Material poverty is also a spiritual problem. The image of God in human form is marred when people are hungry, sick, tormented by demons, or living apart from their Creator. Therefore, our good news for these people must be all the good news.

When Jesus called the twelve disciples, as recorded in Mark, he first called them to "be with him." Being with Jesus is the beginning of life and the beginning of ministry. The disciples were to be with him so that they could preach that people should repent, and so that they could drive out demons and heal the sick. Life, word, sign and deed. Our broken world needs and deserves the whole gospel from whole people.

Good news for the poor

The poor need to hear some good news, if for no other reason than this is what Jesus commands. God's creation is to be productive, made fruitful. We are the ones who are to make it so.

This is not a call for government intervention or redistribution of wealth. It is a call for Christians to go and work alongside those who need support, encouragement, options, access and a little help so that they in turn can make their contribution to God's commandment that all of us be stewards of his creation.

Authentic Christian spirituality

But is our faith up to the task? Christian activists in the inner cities are falling away, burned out by the corrosive influence of sin, size and dynamical relationships confronting those who live in the urban world. Relief workers are collapsing under the weight of too many refugees, horribly abused, their faith eroding in the face of questions about the sovereignty of a God whose creatures commit such horrors.

We cannot transform the world on our own. We do not have the psychological and physical resources in ourselves, or even in our churches. We need to develop a spirituality capable of sustaining us for a lifelong journey in a broken and hostile world.

The rest of the world is also seeking spiritual answers that work. In a postmodern world, the danger is that any spirituality will do. Therefore, our calling demands an authentically Christian spirituality.

A new center of gravity

Everyone knows that the center of gravity of the Christian world has moved to the South into Africa and Latin America and to the East into Asia. Not everyone has adjusted to this fact.

We need to develop an intercontinental conversation that helps identify the gifts God has placed in each continent for the well-being of his global Christian community. Not every continent has the same thing to offer. Yes, the energy and resource for mission is emerging from every continent, and this is good. But when every continent is attempting the same work, this is not so good.

Without all the gifts each continent is uniquely able to offer, the global church is impoverished. Mission work and theological work needs to be done where the church is best able to do it well, on behalf of us all.

Strategic allocation of mission resources

There is enough money for Christian mission in all parts of God's world. However, the way we are allocating our resources for mission continues to be a scandal. The problem is distribution.

Something is wrong when over ninety percent of the church's mission force is working in that part of the world that calls itself Christian. This is not a call to abandon those people groups that are part of the "Christian" world and still have not heard the gospel. It is a call for a more strategic balance. One billion people live where there is little possibility they will ever have a chance to hear about Jesus Christ. They deserve an opportunity to meet a Christian and hear about Christ's claims on their lives.

Twin citizenship

Few today have much faith in the ability of global structures to do anything well that has to be done in local settings. It's simply too far from Colorado Springs, Geneva and Rome to the ministry front lines. No one can see that far.

At the same time, we cannot benefit from economies of scale or the experience of others if our world is limited to the local neighborhood, village, parish or barrio.

Our structures are not keeping up with the changes in the contexts in which they work. The Christian church needs to work away from its hierarchical past and move toward fostering twin citizenship, helping us be citizens of our local churches and their contexts, on the one hand, and citizens of the global church and the world, on the other.

The whole people of God

People are one of the things that have changed most significantly in the last half of this century. People are better educated, and have access to information about their world in ways that were never before possible. More people now have the analytical and conceptual skills to understand what this news means. Many people believe deep inside that their actions can make a difference. People like this are a powerful new force in human history, toppling Marcos, the Berlin wall, the Russian empire and the military dictatorships of Latin America. The list could go on.

This sea change has its parallels in mission work as well. Today, a greater proportion of people are active in mission than ever before. Christian people believe they can make a difference.

Most of these people are volunteers and are not professionally trained in theology or ministry. They are talented, intelligent and committed. Our churches must break with the professional/lay dichotomy and learn how to mobilize and support the whole people of God. These people are our greatest resource and our hope.

A biblical counterpoint

The creation story

By the time Noah was born, God was very unhappy.

God had made a garden, full of animals, fish, plants and trees. He had added something even better, two people made in his own image, the firstborn of creation. Their only job was to enjoy God and tend his garden, to make it productive, to be fruitful, to add a little creativity of their own. Everything in the garden was theirs, except one tree. Apparently, they had not been made to handle the knowledge of good and evil.

But they ate of the one tree they were not given, and God, as a God of justice, had to act. To protect them, they were asked to leave the Garden and were kept from returning on their own. For Adam and Eve, things natural to them became harder and more painful. But, even outside the garden, God remained with them.

Then the story gets sadder. One of their sons killed the other because he could not handle disappointment, apparently unwilling to let God be God. When Cain is asked where his brother is, he says he does not know. God replies, "Your brother's blood cries out to me from the ground."

Again God, who is just, must act. Cain is made a wanderer, a refugee; the ground will not yield its crops to him. Cain is afraid; he is sure he will be killed. Not even God's mark of protection reassures Cain.

The wanderer begins to build cities, permanent places with walls for protection. From his line, we learn of the emergence of livestock, music, metal tools — the hallmarks of emerging civilization. Cain and his descendants are going to take care of themselves. They are still hard at work today, as convinced as ever that they can create a just and peaceful world without God's help.

By the time Noah is born, things have gotten very bad indeed. "Every inclination of their hearts was only evil all the time," said God of humankind. We are told that God was grieved and that his heart was filled with pain. God decided to wipe it all out — humankind, animals, creatures that move along the ground and birds of the air: "I am grieved that I have made them."

It seemed God's creation story was coming to an early, disappointing end. Only then do we learn of Noah, a righteous man. Because God saw this man's righteousness, Noah, his family, and a remnant of all living things, will be saved. The great flood came, destroying everything — all except Noah, his extended family and those God told to join him on the ark.

With that event, this sad story becomes hopeful once again. God decides he will never destroy humankind again, in spite of the fact that human nature has not changed: "Never again will I curse the ground because of man, even though every inclination of his heart is evil from childhood. And never again will I destroy all living creatures."

Grieving the heart of God

Too often this story is read as a legal story, a story of trials and penalties. And it is that to some degree. God has rules, and we are supposed to obey them. When we don't, there are consequences, serious ones. God is a God of justice, after all.

But there is more to the story and we need to hear this part, too. God's reaction was caused by what he felt, not by a list of rules that were broken. His heart was grieved. The flood story is about emotions, about relationships, about feelings. God felt pain. We need to think hard about what it was that grieved God's heart so.

First, God must have felt disappointment that his creation seemed so insistent in turning against his purposes for it. Surely God's pain over this continues today. Today's world is clearly a creation still bent on going its own way, stubbornly seeking to exclude God and the idea of God from its concern.

Even more compelling, the blood of violence cries out to God from the ground. For God, killing is a loud, painful, attention-getting act. The world we've just glimpsed in this booklet is a world full of violence, strife, people being hurt, abused, misused and killed. If God heard the cry of the spilt blood of one innocent man, how much more so must his heart be grieved today?

What can we learn from this story?

First, our God is a relational God before and after he is a just God. In his creation, he created relationships before he established a rule.

Even after his rule was broken, his grace superseded his justice. "If you eat of the tree you will die," he said. But Adam and Eve did not die. Even when Cain had killed and deserved death, God spared him and then offered to guarantee his safety. In a world that fully warranted being wiped out, God found one righteous man and decided to sustain his creation in spite of its overwhelming failure.

Today we know the rest of the story; grace and relationships take precedence over sin and judgment. If you are in relationship with his Son, your sin is forgiven.

Our Christian mission must build on this truth. Our ministry must be one of restored relationships, of reconciliation. People need to be invited to be reconciled with God, with their inner selves, with their fellow human beings and with the world God created to be their home.

Our ministry must be relational before it is anything else. The only two commandments Christ gave us are both relational: Love your God and love your neighbor. Loving people who do not deserve or attract love must be the basis of Christian mission in today's world.

The second lesson is that there is always at least one righteous person somewhere in the midst of evil. Noah was there. Abraham convinced God to spare Sodom and Gomorrah on the basis of a handful of righteous people. We are all offered life, instead of the death our sin deserves, because there was one who was perfect before God.

Mission at the end of this century takes place in situations where sin and evil appear to have the upper hand. The inner cities of the West, the refugee camps full of those who have seen their loved ones butchered, the women and children who have experienced things too evil to mention.

Many feel as if sin has had the final say. God's story declares that this is not true. Somewhere in the midst of people whose only inclination is evil, we will find a Noah if we look hard enough. In Christian ministry at the end of this century, we need to look for the Noahs and, like God, begin our search for transformation with them.

Finally, we learn that in the end God made a conscious decision not to give up.

After the flood, nothing had changed. Even though he was starting with righteous Noah and his three sons and their families, we are told that every inclination of their hearts is "evil from childhood." Yet God decided to stick it out, to call Abraham, to choose Israel, to exile Israel, to protect a remnant and finally to provide the answer to human sin through the finished work of his Son on the cross.

In our ministry in the midst of a world that must pain and grieve the heart of God no less now than before, we must not give up. God hasn't.

We need to ask God for the faith and spirituality to embrace the pain and injustice of this world, and keep going.

Even when it appears we are making no difference, we must believe that the vision of a world with God and without tears is God's final word.

Bibliography

Barrett, David. "Annual Statistical Tables on Global Mission: 1995," *International Bulletin of Missionary Research.* January 1995.

Barrett, David. "Annual Statistical Tables on Global Mission: 1996," *International Bulletin of Missionary Research.* January 1996.

Barrett, David and Todd Johnson. *AD2000 Global Monitor.* January 1993.

Barrett, David and Todd Johnson. *AD2000 Global Monitor.* January 1994.

Barrett, David and Todd Johnson. *AD2000 Global Monitor.* April 1994.

Barrett, David and Todd Johnson. *AD2000 Global Monitor.* October 1994.

Barrett, David and Todd Johnson. *AD2025 Global Monitor.* September 1995.

Barrett, David and Todd Johnson. *Our Globe and How to Reach It.* Birmingham: New Hope, 1990.

Brierley, Peter. *UK Christian Handbook 1992-93.* London: MARC Europe, 1992.

Bosch, David. *Transforming Mission: Paradigm Shifts in Theology of Mission.* Maryknoll: Orbis, 1991.

Bread for the World. *Hunger 1996: Countries in Crisis.* Silver Spring, MD: Bread for the World, 1995.

Cairncross, Frances. "The Death of Distance: A Survey of Telecommunications," *The Economist.* September 30, 1995.

Carter Center. *State of the World Conflict Report 1994-1995.* Atlanta: The Carter Center, 1995.

Duffield, Mark. "Complex Emergencies and the Crisis of Developmentalism," *IDS Bulletin*, Vol. 25, No. 4, 1994

Economist, The. "Pity the Children." August 31, 1996.

Greeley, Andrew. "Religion Around the World: A Preliminary Report." Chicago: NORC, 1992.

Gwartney, James; Robert Lawson and Walter Block. *Economic Freedom of the World 1975-1995.* Vancouver: Fraser Institute, 1996.

ICVA and Eurostep, *The Reality of Aid: An Independent Review of International Aid.* London: Earthscan Publications, Ltd., 1996.

Johnstone, Patrick. *Operation World.* Grand Rapids: Zondervan, 1993.

Kidron, Michael and Ronald Segal. *The State of the World Atlas.* London: Penguin, 1995.

Lapple, Alfred. *The Catholic Church: A Brief History.* New York: Paulist Press, 1982.

Linthicum, Robert C. *Empowering the Poor.* Monrovia: MARC, 1991.

Mata, Francisco; Larry Onisto and J.R. Vallentyne. "Consumption: The Other Side of Population for Development," paper prepared for the International Conference on Population and Development. Cairo, 1994.

Medecins sans Frontieres. *Populations in Danger.* London: John Libby, 1992.

Myers, Bryant. *The Changing Shape of World Mission.* Monrovia: MARC, 1993.

Myers, Bryant. "State of the World's Children," *International Bulletin of Missionary Research.* July 1994.

Nasar, Sylvia. "Economics of Equality: A New View," *New York Times.* January 5, 1996.

Neill, Stephen. *A History of Christian Missions.* New York: Penguin, 1964.

Parker, John. "Turn Up the Lights: A Survey of Cities," *The Economist.* July 29, 1995.

Persson, Torsten and Guido Tabellini. "Is Inequality Harmful for Growth?" *American Economic Review.* June 1994.

Pollack, Andrew. "A Cyberspace Front in a Multicultural War," *New York Times.* August 7, 1995.

Population Reference Bureau. "1995 World Population Data Sheet." Washington D.C., 1995.

Seager, Joni. *The State of the Earth Atlas.* New York: Touchstone/Simon and Schuster, 1990.

Seager, Joni. *The New State of the Earth Atlas.* New York: Touchstone/Simon and Schuster, 1995.

UNDP, *Human Development Report 1995.* New York: Oxford University Press, 1995.

UNHCR, *The State of the World's Refugees 1995: In Search of Solutions.* New York: Oxford University Press, 1995.

UNICEF, *State of the World's Children 1995.* New York: Oxford University Press, 1995.

Walls, Andrew. "The Old Age of the Missionary Movement." *International Review of Mission.* LXVI Jan. 1987.

Walls, Andrew. "The Significance of Christianity in Africa," public lecture at St. Colm's Education Centre and College, 21 May 1989.

World Resources Institute. *World Resources 1994-1995.* New York: Oxford University Press, 1994.

World Vision UK. "Children At Risk." (Milton Keyes, UK, 1992).

More Key Mission Resources from MARC

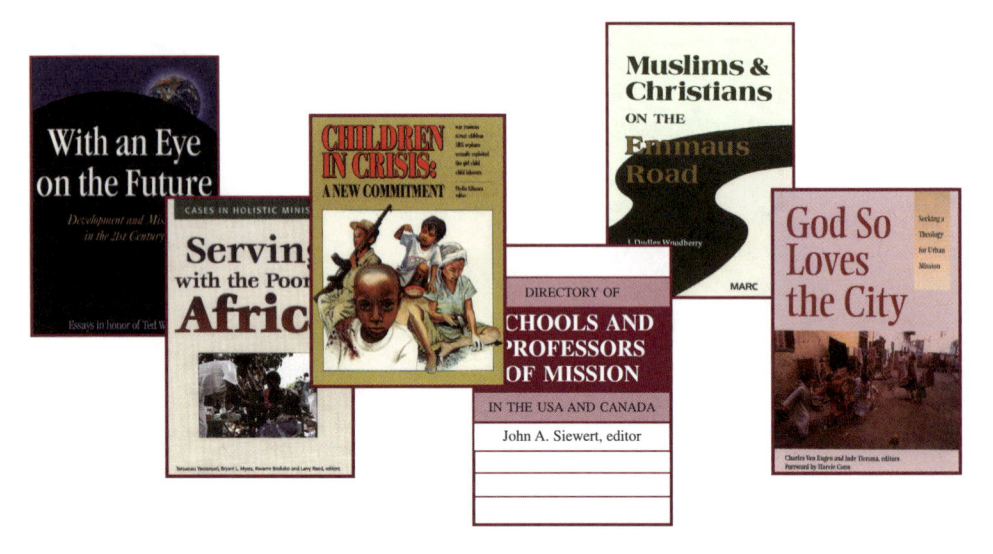

WITH AN EYE ON THE FUTURE
Development and Mission in the 21st Century
Duane Elmer and Lois McKinney, editors
Examines four areas that will be critical to mission in the 21st century: theological education, global mission, international development and church leadership. 272 pp. $24.95

SERVING WITH THE POOR IN AFRICA
Cases in Holistic Ministry
T. Yamamori, B. Myers, K. Bediako and L. Reed, editors
From several different African contexts come fascinating new case studies and analyses on the nature of holistic mission. 240 pp. $15.95

CHILDREN IN CRISIS
A New Commitment
Phyllis Kilbourn, editor
Acquaints you with the many crises children are facing today and equips you for a biblical response. 304 pp. $21.95

DIRECTORY OF SCHOOLS AND PROFESSORS OF MISSION IN THE USA AND CANADA
John A. Siewert, editor
Your complete networking tool for mission schools and faculty in North America. All the contact information you'll need. 124 pp. $11.95

MUSLIMS AND CHRISTIANS ON THE EMMAUS ROAD
J. Dudley Woodberry, editor
The starting point for effective witness to Muslims today. Helps you understand the crucial issues involved. 392 pp. $15.95

GOD SO LOVES THE CITY
Seeking a Theology for Urban Mission
Charles Van Engen and Jude Tiersma, editors
An international team of urban practitioners explores the critical issues facing those who minister in today's cities. 315 pp. $21.95

Ask for the complete publications catalog and free MARC newsletter

MARC 800 W. Chestnut Ave. • Monrovia, CA • 91016-3198 • USA
Direct: (818) 301-7720 • Fax: (818) 301-7786 • E-mail: MARCpubs@wvi.org

1-800-777-7752

In a world with so much need, what can one person do? For that matter, what difference can a group or church make? plenty

World Vision has developed a variety of ways for individuals, groups, and churches to get personally involved in helping people in need. By partnering with people like you, we are able to provide long-term, sustainable development and emergency relief to millions of people around the world and in the United States every year. **It all starts one person at a time. The following pages are devoted to helping you, your group, or your church become involved in making a world of difference.**

30 Hour Famine

The 30 Hour Famine is an unforgettable event that brings participants together with their friends and over 1 million others worldwide to help hurting children. Here's how:

Participants find people to sponsor them for the 30 hours they go without food. While experiencing firsthand the reality of hunger, participants also learn about the issues of hunger and proverty through materials and activities provided free by World Vision. Then the money they raise and send to World Vision helps feed hungry and starving children around the world.

It's a simple concept that involved over 300,000 students and others in 1996. And the money they raised enabled participants to be personally responsible for helping feed over 21,000 children for an entire year!

The national **30 Hour Famine** dates are always the last weekend in February. But your group can do the Famine anytime! Just do the Famine and help save kids' lives! **Sign up and get a free video by calling 1-800-7FAMINE (1-800-732-6463).** Check out the 30 Hour Famine Web site at http://www.30hourfamine.org.

Child Sponsorship

Child Sponsorship is a way you or your group can help break the cycle of poverty and famine by beginning a life-changing relationship with a needy child. It's a practical way to provide opportunities for health, nutrition and education for a child, along with the possibility of self-reliance for the child's community.

It only takes $20 a month, or 50¢ a day, to share the hope of a better life—and the opportunity to know of Christ's love—with a hurting child and his or her community.

When you sponsor a child, you will receive a photo and information about your child. You also will have the opportunity to correspond with him or her. Become a child sponsor today and make a difference in the life of a child forever.

For more information on sponsoring a child, call 1-800-7FAMINE (1-800-732-6463).

partnering with peop
world of difference he

● Indicates World Vision program site.

LOVE INC

Are you and your church looking for more effective ways to meet the needs of your community? Do you want to help but are not sure how to go about it? LOVE INC, short for Love In the Name of Christ, is a strategy that enables church volunteers to help their neighbors in need. LOVE INC, a ministry of World Vision, acts as a clearinghouse to mobilize volunteers from local churches to work cooperatively with public and private agencies in meeting the needs of local people. The LOVE INC program provides direct and tangible ways for willing volunteers to express their concern for needy families. More than 3,300 churches are associated with LOVE INC, representing a diverse group that includes over 100 denominations in 96 communities in more than 30 states.

For more information about LOVE INC, please call 1-800-777-5277.

Project Home Again

You can help bring a family "home" by becoming involved in this six-month mentoring program. Project Home Again trains churches and volunteers to help homeless families become self-sufficient. Caring and skilled church volunteers lend support to those in need by helping find and furnish housing, providing guidance with budgeting and financial planning, securing stable employment, and helping with personal care issues. To volunteer or for more information, call 206-815-2078.

Love For Children

The majority of needy people in the United States are women and children. Early, caring intervention is critically needed in the lives of disadvantaged children if they are to have a chance at escaping poverty's downward spiral. Love For Children is making a difference by mobilizing churches and volunteers to help children at risk and their families. Serving as a clearinghouse organization, this program works closely with two federal programs, Head Start and Women, Infants and Children (WIC), to identify children at risk and provide donated goods and volunteer services to local families.

For more information, call 616-392-8277 or e-mail: LFC@loveforchildren.org. LFC's WWW home page: http://www.loveforchildren.org

everywhere to make a
at home

CityLinc

Each day the headlines are filled with alarming stories of life in the inner city. You may ask yourself, "What is being done to help?" and "How can I get involved?" Through World Vision's CityLinc program, volunteers are connected with community-based non-profits and church-based ministries in the inner city that need your help as they seek to build and rehabilitate homes, feed the hungry, plant flowers and trees, and mentor and tutor kids in the community. The opportunities are limitless. The CityLinc program is currently active in Chicago and the District of Columbia.

For more information call 202-547-3743 (Washington, D.C.) or 312-322-3000 (Chicago).

Countertop Partners

Countertop Partners help by placing collection displays in local businesses where small contributions add up to a significant amount of help for a needy world. When an earthquake hits, a famine occurs, or any other emergency arises, World Vision is there with immediate help, thanks in part to this nationwide network of partners.

To sign up or to find out more information, call toll free 1-800-444-2522 (English) and 1-800-522-9888 (Spanish).

Love Loaf

Love Loaves are coin collection banks that churches distribute to families to take home and fill. At the end of one month, the coin-filled loaves are brought back to church and sent to World Vision to support food, health, agriculture, and evangelism programs. Churches may choose to keep up to 50 percent of the total amount raised for their local mission projects.

To sign up or to find out more information, call toll free 1-800-444-2522.

World Vision Volunteer Network

The World Vision Volunteer Network is made up of people from across the country who are trained and supported by regional managers to be a Child Sponsorship Representative, 30 Hour Famine Representative, Countertop Representative, or a World Vision Representative working with all three programs. Depending on the desired level of involvement, there are many ways to serve as a Volunteer Networking Representative.

To get involved or find out more information, call one of our regional offices at 1-800-787-4687 (East Coast), 1-800-967-9999 (Midwest), or 1-800-340-2214 (West Coast).